THE BALANCED LIFE

Dr. Barbara McFarland

Bloomington, IN Milton Keynes, UK

authorHOUSE®

AuthorHouse™
1663 Liberty Drive, Suite 200
Bloomington, IN 47403
www.authorhouse.com
Phone: 1-800-839-8640

AuthorHouse™ UK Ltd.
500 Avebury Boulevard
Central Milton Keynes, MK9 2BE
www.authorhouse.co.uk
Phone: 08001974150

First published by AuthorHouse 10/10/2006

ISBN: 1-4208-7690-2 (sc)

Library of Congress Control Number: 2005907247

Printed in the United States of America
Bloomington, Indiana

This book is printed on acid-free paper.

Also by Dr. Barbara McFarland

Feeding the Empty Heart

Shame and Body Image
Co-author Tyeis Baker Baumann

Finding the Adult Within

Brief Therapy & Eating Disorders
(English and Japanese)

My Mother Was Right!
Co-author Virginia W. Rouslin
(English and Taiwanese)

Take Back Your Life NOW!
Co-author Steve Wuest

To
The men in my life,
Harold & Casey
And the boys,
Todd, Chad & Gavin

And last but not least
To my sister,
Charley

Acknowledgements

With each book I write, I am always amazed at the support I receive. As with the other books, my greatest support has been my husband, Harold. As my editor, over the course of the project, he has been brutal, kind, gentle, and justifiably critical. More importantly, as I have holed myself up in my office for hours, days and week-ends, he has never complained about my absence and always inquired about my progress. He is the author behind the author.

Although there have been many, I'd like to deeply thank the women at Procter & Gamble who have supported my work especially *Helayne Angelus, Deb Barrett, Hanan Heikal, Gale Beckett, Kristine Mauro and Mary Anne Gale*. They have been an inspiration to me. They serve as incredible role-models to the women at Procter &Gamble and are true change agents. Deep appreciation also goes to Virginia Watson Rouslin, my co-author on *My Mother Was Right!* and Dr. Pamela Graber for the opportunity to work with them on Anthem Blue Cross Blue Shield Healthy Woman's Program and for introducing me to Nancy Girton, who continues to support my work at Anthem and beyond. My creative genius, Alta Bradford has always been a phone call away and did a wonderful job on the cover of this book.

Most of all, I am grateful to all of the women over the past 25 years who have trusted me with their deepest secrets, sorrows and sufferings. They have come into my life in times of crisis and leave more deeply connected to their inner strengths – that which was there before they passed through my door. They will never know that they gave me far more than I ever gave them. They have inspired me, lightened my own burdens with their humor and resilience and added a richness to my life. My dear women, you are the heroines of my life.

Contents

Learn to be silent.
Let your
Quiet mind
Listen and absorb.

Pythagoras
(580 BC – 500 BC)

All man's miseries derive from not being
able to sit quietly in a room alone.

Blaise Pascal
(1623 – 1662)

Every now and then go away,
        have a little relaxation,
        for when you come back
        to your work
        your judgement will be surer;
        since to remain constantly at work
        will cause you to lose power
        of judgement…

Go some distance away
        because the work appears smaller
        and more of it
        can be taken in at a glance
        and a lack of harmony
        or proportion
        is more readily seen.

Leonardo Da Vinci
(1452 –1519)

Forward
Second Edition

Since the first printing of *The Balanced Life*, I have presented the *Flex*Life seminar to many groups of working women throughout the US, in Asia and in South America. As a result of these sessions and the feedback I have received from participants, I realized that I needed to enhance the content of this book in several ways, thus, the revised Second Edition.

First, I've expanded the section for single people addressing more of their needs. I've revamped the Personal Resources Quadrant to include Nine Personal Qualities which are clinically based and more comprehensive than the Ten Traits. The other added content deals with men. I have repeatedly heard, "What about the men in our lives? They need balance, too!"

Although I have primarily worked with women both in my private practice and in the corporate arena, I have had clinical experience with the challenges men face in their own personal and professional lives. (Being married for 25 years and raising a son has given me many great personal insights.) I've come to this awareness at crisis points in men's lives. Unlike women who view counseling as helpful and supportive, men think of counselors as they do of dentists – "Go only if in excruciating never-ending unceasing pain." So, I've dealt with men at their worst times -- when a marriage or relationship is falling apart or a job is lost. And I never get to know them for very long because once the problem is solved or resolved they're off and running. Sometimes they're off and running regardless. Not that that's a bad thing but as someone who promotes behavioral and attitudinal change, I know that it often times takes *time* to do a little bit of soul searching and self-examination to learn from a loss or life changing event. But of course, that's from a woman's perspective!

The good news is that I have found this style of problem resolution to be changing for men ages 26 and 40 commonly referred to as Generation X. They are concerned about the ongoing *quality* of their lives and want to develop attitudes and behaviors that will enhance their personal and professional relationships; therefore, they are willing to dig deeper in order to understand their own decisions and actions. This group wants a better quality of life.

Consequently life balance is becoming increasingly important for men as well as women. No longer willing to be passive or absent in their significant relationships, men are seeking to be more participatory and involved. They are taking on more and more responsibilities on the home front. According to the Equal Opportunities Commission, a surprising 36% of couples say that the man is the main caretaker while women are working more. In another study conducted by the Families and Work Institute in New York, a nonprofit that tracks trends in family life, fathers in 2002 spent 2.7 hours each workday caring for children, almost an hour more than fathers in 1977. That reflects a 50 percent increase in male participation. During the same 25-year period, working mothers' hours spent caring for children stayed roughly the same - 3.3 hours a day. Polls also show that fathers feel they are missing out on time with their children.

Although this is good news, many men are reluctant to admit to having life balance issues. They lack the confidence, tools and language to negotiate their personal and family needs with their managers. In many organizations it's not as acceptable for men to take time off to care for elderly parents or bond with a new born infant as it is for women. So they are disinclined to ask for more flexible working hours or to simply leave early to attend a kid's soccer tournament. They are often driven to lie rather than to risk appearing to be less committed than their male counter-parts and managers.

An organizational culture that takes its cue from the more traditional division of labor has to be changed because most work cultures expect people to leave their personal selves at the door. Employees feel they have to hide parts of themselves or split off their childcare needs, relationship issues, etc. From a psychological standpoint, when we have to "split off" or deny parts of ourselves, we experience a schizophrenic quality of life. Our energy is fragmented. Our productivity is diminished. Respecting the whole person, valuing his/her total life is the heart of diversity.

Challenges for Women

Although we want our spouses and partners to participate more in household responsibilities and child/eldercare, we women sometimes have a difficult time letting go and frequently believe that "My partner can't do it as well as I can." I often share a personal experience of my own in dealing with this challenge.

Some years ago, I was having a particularly tough day – most of my clients were experiencing some difficult problems and one of them was suicidal which was particularly draining. On my way home from the office, I began to go through my mental checklist of what I would prepare for dinner, what I had in the fridge and what errands I had to run. I needed to go to the grocery to pick up a few things, go to the bank for my husband and then to the cleaners to pick up a pair of slacks my son had to have for a social event. When I got home, I got dinner going, set the table, and did a load of laundry. While I was cooking over a hot stove with perspiration dripping from my brow, I glanced over into the family room and lo and behold! There was my husband and son having a grand time watching television passing the remote between them.

Well, I had an out-of-body experience! I stormed over, grabbed the remote and looked at the two of them with fire in my eyes and shouted, "I QUIT!" With that I walked out of the house, got into my car, drove to one of the finest restaurants in town and ordered a glass of wine. With a smile on my face, I placed that remote on the plate right across from me!

Now, several days later, after the initial freeze wore off, my husband approached me and said, "You know, I realize that you have a point here. However, in fairness to us whenever we have tried to do the laundry or cook you have been very critical – it's never been good enough. And most of the time you never ask for help or tell us what you need. So, how about if we call a truce and you first let us know what you need and, secondly, understand that we're not going to do it exactly the way YOU would do it."

Well, I had to admit he was right. One interesting thing about being a psychologist and hearing the life challenges that people face is that I've come to learn just how similar we all are. As I heard my husband share his feelings I had flashbacks of sessions with couples I've worked with – those very words were spoken by a number of men who accompanied their wives to therapy.

So, women, we need to communicate clearly and directly as to what we need and, no, most men aren't going to anticipate what should be done around the house or what the kids need the way we do. I chalk it up to socialization and some biology – but they are teachable and, in fact, younger men coming up *are* tuned in much more to household responsibilities and childcare issues. The other factor is that we have to let what they do be "good enough." They have their own way of doing things and we need to adjust our standards and methods if we're going to have true partners. And, men, don't use your partner's different standards or criticisms as an excuse not to pitch in – those differences need to be discussed and negotiated. That way, the whole family can experience some degree of balance. Being sensitive to diversity means you're aware of biological and personal differences with all those in your life.

Marie, a thirty-nine-year-old mother of two always picked up the children at daycare every day after work. When her husband got a new job which changed his nine to five work day to seven to three, she continued to pick up the kids even though he was home a few hours earlier than she. She sought counseling because she had a melt-down when, after picking up the kids, she came home to find him taking a nap! During one of our sessions I suggested that she turn this responsibility over to him. It never entered her mind to do this. "But I don't know if I can depend on him." I said, "Well, it's about time you found out." She did and although at first he was reluctant, he became the star dad at the day care center.

Many men are willing but lack the confidence to cross over the traditional role boundaries. So, we have to coach them and communicate clearly what's needed to run a healthy, balanced household.

Benefits to Men

So, although many of the concepts in this book are based on female life balance challenges, I know men can benefit as well. However, I ask that my male audience be tolerant of my phraseology – I realize men may not particularly relate to the phrase "being present" as they most likely would prefer "being focused." I know "creating "space" might be considered something too fluffy and nebulous and the male brain would relate better to "make the time." Well, bear with those female nuances of language and be creative in applying the concepts to your experience for I am confident all of the content in this book will serve you well.

At many of my keynotes I've had men in the audience and, without fail, I am always approached by two or three thanking me for giving them insight into their wives, sisters, partners, and mothers. So, this book can really give men a new perspective on the women in their lives -- Chapter Four is particularly eye-opening for men. Read that one for the women in your lives—it will give you the **_secret_** to understanding us.

In addition, the book itself will give men a conceptual framework upon which to assesses their current stage of balance and provide them with some tools to develop a behaviorally based action plan. Additionally, I've invited two successful married men at different life stages with children to offer their perspectives on life balance: Mike Friedman, a manager at Procter & Gamble, married father of two and Dave Homan, a marketing executive, married father of 3. I chose Mike and Dave because I know they walk the walk and have made tough choices to achieve balance in their lives. I'm certain their messages will resonate with all who read them.

Even though there are significant differences between men and women, I also know that the similarities are even greater. We all want to be loved at home and valued on the job regardless of what sex we are. It's that simple. The methods for getting these needs met are approached by men and women in diverse ways but the bottom line remains the same.

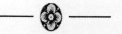

Introduction

When I was a single mom, taking care of my son, working full time and going to school in order to realize my dream of becoming a psychologist, I remember feeling frazzled and frequently overwhelmed, and I would have waves of guilt wash over me daily because I turned much of the care of my son over to my parents while I worked and continued with my studies. Getting up at 4:00 AM and collapsing in bed at midnight was the norm.

In the 1970s, for most women, having a "balanced life" wasn't even a part of their vocabulary -- survival was. So, I was trying to survive as a mother, an employee, a graduate student and a graduate teaching assistant. Whew! Even without cell phones, e-mails, laptops, voicemails, blackberries and all the other technological devices that have cluttered our lives since then, I look back and remember that time as a whirring buzz of doings and comings and goings.

Here I am now, twenty plus years later and the only major difference in my life is that my son has grown into a fine young man. I'm still a whirring buzz of doings and comings and goings; however, the whirring buzz isn't controlling me anymore -- I'm controlling it and that's what this book is all about.

Sick and Tired of Being Sick and Tired

As I look back at the issues women have sought counseling for over the past 20+ years, I have seen some interesting trends. In the1980s and early to mid 1990s, women were more focused on glass ceiling issues, not only having to adapt to masculine leadership styles at the expense of their own natural styles but also learning to understand and value their feminine work and leadership styles. In addition, they had to concentrate on their struggles with the relationships in their lives, generally focusing on communication, appropriate boundaries and co-dependency issues. Although these topics are still of concern to women, something else surfaced that significantly overshadowed them.

In the mid-1990s, I began to hear women say, "I'm exhausted and overwhelmed. I feel so off balance." "I have to get some balance in my life." As women crossed into the new millennium, they began questioning the quality of their lives. "I feel like I'm sacrificing my family for my job. How can I be more balanced?" "I need a life!" "Why do *I* have to do it all?"

In response to the increasing stress levels women experience as a result of their multiple roles and responsibilities, many are leaving their jobs to start their own businesses, seeking jobs with less responsibilities or making financial sacrifices to stay at home -- steps taken to insure their flexibility and autonomy so they can "have a life." And thus the phrase "work/life balance" has become embedded into the psyche of women everywhere.

Through my own personal experiences and my work with women, I have discovered that experiencing a balanced life is pretty simple. "Simple," you ask incredulously? Yes. Simple. "Nothing is simple," you say.

Well, there is some truth to this. And if experiencing a balanced life were too simple, we'd question its validity. As human beings we like complexity. The more difficult something is the more it intrigues us. If we have to work hard at something, we value it more. And if the truth be known, although my discovery is simple, integrating it into our lives is definitely not!

In the last few years I have been exploring, researching and developing tools and strategies that can help people improve the quality of their lives. As a result, I designed a work/life balance seminar called *FlexLife: Choices and Strategies* and have delivered it throughout the U.S and in Asia. This book is based on that seminar and includes all of the key concepts contained within it.

This book is intended to be an ongoing support and reinforcement to the *Flex*Life seminar although it isn't necessary to have attended a seminar to benefit from the book.

I suggest you get together with your partner, spouse or other women and discuss the ideas and concepts presented, supporting each other as you integrate these learnings into your daily lives. Many who have attended my seminars have commented that sharing ideas and giving and receiving support was the most effective part of the day. Again, since our schedules are packed so tightly, we frequently procrastinate getting together with friends or making time to converse with our partners. Use this book as way as to help stay on the "balanced life" track and/or to support one another in the pursuit of a more balanced life.

One

— ❀ —

To Be or Not To Be

"Most people die at age 25. They just don't get buried until they're 65."
Ben Franklin

When pressed about the greatest work/life balance struggle they have to deal with, many people complain that they need more time. "If only there were more hours in a day, I could do it all." "There's too much to do with so little time."

Actually, time is NOT the major problem in being able to balance our lives. Research was conducted surveying 800 graduates of two business schools in Pennsylvania on the challenges of work/life balance. Survey respondents felt that the psychological conflicts that come from thinking about work when at home and thinking about home when at work are more of an issue than time. How often have you fretted over a family issue while you were attending a departmental meeting? How frequently have you tuned out your family while you were mentally preparing for a presentation? These types of conflicts are often followed by waves of guilt and self-recrimination.

Susan, a 40 year-old single mother of twin boys age 10, sought me out after a keynote presentation I did in Tacoma, Washington. "I feel like a ping pong ball most of the time. When I'm at work, I'm often distracted because I feel terribly guilty I'm not spending enough time with my boys. And then when I AM home with them, I'm obsessed with picking up my e-mails and voicemails so that I don't get behind at work. I feel like a failure as a mom and as a manager."

The Addiction to Doing

So we end up living our lives on a hamster wheel that keeps going faster and faster -- so much so that we move through our lives and our relationships in a trance. We go through the motions but we're not really *there*. We're not present. We're not focused on what is happening in the here and now.

We have become addicted to busyness. I've seen people having conversations while checking their e-mails on their blackberries (often jokingly referred to as crackberries). I have watched women become crazed as they whirl through McDonald's having a "family" dinner in the car while driving their kids to some soccer game or ballet lesson all the while shoveling food in at warp speed. When I've been talking on the phone with colleagues or clients, words I hear sputter out in between the slurping of a Coke and the chomping of a sandwich while in the background there is a clicking of nails on a keyboard. We call this "multi-tasking" and view it as a special talent of women. I call it "addicti-tasking" and view it as unhealthy and very unproductive.

Throughout my career I've worked with people suffering from substance addictions – drugs, alcohol and food. Recently, I've added another one to the list -- the "doing" addiction. An addiction, any addiction, keeps the addicted individual from connecting with her inner experience -- from her feelings. It keeps her from being present in her own life and in her relationships with others.

Beth Ann, a thirty-eight-year-old single mother of two girls ages 15 and 13 best illustrates my point. When Beth Ann first came to see me, I was struck by how "perfect" she looked. It was as if she stepped off a page in More magazine. As she sat on my couch folding her arms tightly across her chest, I noticed how stiff and tense her body was. With pursed lips and rapid fire speech, she told me she was seeking counseling because she needed to get more balance and control in her life. She took out her Franklin Planner (the pages of which had no white space left) and handed me an agenda for our session. This was a first for me but having been a therapist for all these years, nothing I see or hear surprises me.

She took charge of the session going over each item while I sat and listened. My usual therapy style is a very interactive one but with Beth Ann, there was no way to get a word in edgewise. It took no time at all to determine that she was a doing addict – working full time as a VP of a major hospital, going to school part time, managing her house like boot camp and running her girls hither and yon.

Sessions continued for several months and each time she brought a detailed agenda and each time I complied. During these sessions as she chattered about relatively inconsequential matters, I picked up on sound bytes of anger, depression and fear related to her daughter's severe depression which resulted in several hospitalizations. Whenever I tried to explore these feelings, Beth Ann quickly reminded me we were not on task!

One day as I went to greet her in the waiting room, I noticed that she was visibly upset and her appearance was somewhat disheveled. When she plopped down on the couch, she looked frantic as the tears spilled over and trickled down her cheeks. "What's happened," I asked? "My God. I lost my planner! I lost my planner!" the weeping turned to sobbing. "I feel so lost. What will we talk about?"

"How wonderful," I thought. "Now, therapy will begin." Finally, Beth Ann was able to connect with her feelings—something she had been desperately avoiding. Without her usual props, she was vulnerable. "I feel like I've failed in some way. Maybe if I had been a better mom, she would be happier." We dug into her feelings about her daughter's illness, which she personalized as her failure as a mother. She was finally able to come to terms with the fact that her mother and grandmother suffered from severe depressive episodes which lessened her guilt considerably.

Achieve vs. Experience

During my sessions, at seminars and at keynotes, attendees will often ask, "How can I achieve a more balanced life?" I tell them there's no way they can achieve balance to which they say, "Then why are you talking about this if you're not going to tell us how to achieve it?"

This idea of "achieving" a balanced life is a very dangerous one for two reasons: first, it sounds like another task or something that we need to add to our "to do" lists; secondly, it implies that balance is an event—something we can get to if we're smart enough or organized enough or read enough self-help books. This notion of achieving balance keeps the hamster wheel spinning even faster, yet any sense of achievement becomes even more illusive.

I tell people that I can help them *experience* a more balanced life. *Experiencing* a balanced life is all about *being*.

The Doing of It All

I look at balance as having two dimensions. The horizontal dimension is the *Doing* Dimension. This is where we live our lives: working, taking care of family, running the household, maintaining a support system, taking care of ourselves, etc. On this dimension, we're generally living in one of two zones: The Rear View Mirror Zone where all we do is think about the past. "I should have told my boss I didn't completely agree with my performance appraisal." "Why did I let Stevie sign up for soccer when he's playing two other sports?" "I wonder if they thought my presentation was thorough?" And so it goes. Mental chatter about what you should have, would have or could have done differently.

The other zone is the Fast Forward Zone where all we think about is the future. "I can't wait for our vacation to come." "I wonder if I'll have enough money to retire on." "What if I can't find another job?"

So our thoughts relentlessly shuttle us back and forth between what "should" or "could have been" to the "what ifs." "I should have told my co-worker that I wasn't in agreement with the direction the team was taking." "I could have been more assertive." "What if I don't get that promotion?" Couple that with grocery lists, gift lists for holidays and family birthdays, anniversaries, lists about lists, along with the other things we have to do like laundry, grocery shopping, cleaning, etc., etc., the Doing Dimension can be all consuming. Actually, it becomes addictive. As it spins out of control, we desperately try to figure out how to gain control and *achieve* a more balanced life.

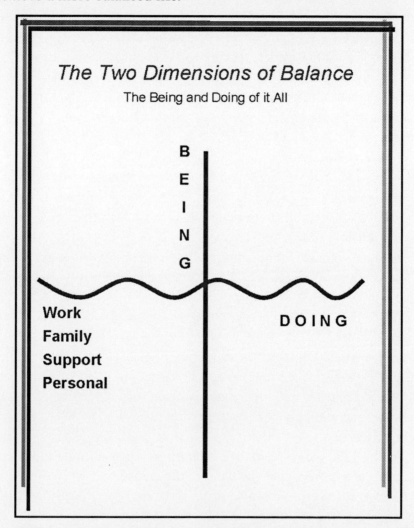

In our efforts to *achieve* balance, we often look outside ourselves and try to change or control others. This leads to anger and resentment and puts a profound strain on relationships.

Kaitlin, an attractive thirty-five-year-old mother of four approached me after a keynote address I delivered in Parsippany, New Jersey. She shared with me that her spouse of twelve years contributed little to the family other than financially. It became clear very quickly that Kaitlin was a perfectionist and frequently criticized her spouse when he would do the laundry or feed the kids as not having done anything the "right way." "If only he would do what I'd ask, I know I wouldn't be so stressed and my life would feel more balanced." Whenever I asked her what she could do differently to improve the situation she repeatedly blamed her spouse and didn't see that she had any responsibility in the matter. When I suggested that she look at her perfectionism as a contributing factor to the problem, she looked startled, then at her watch and said, "I'm late for a meeting. I have to go."

Focusing on what others need to do differently or how our employer could be more supportive as we strive toward balance keeps us stuck and fuels negativity. Examining our own behavior and taking responsibility for what we want is a key underpinning to having a balanced life.

Looking outside of ourselves as we continually become mired in the demands of the doing dimension keeps us forever feeling off kilter.

The Being of It All

The Vertical Dimension – the Being Dimension is the only place we can *experience* balance. When I ask people what balance feels like they equate it with a feeling of peace or centeredness. *Being* means living with a greater sense of presence. It means being *there* in our lives.

In the 1980s, as a result of research on stress and its impact on the body, most everyone who went to the doctor with any complaint from migraines to ingrown toenails were told the malady was the result of too much stress. So, "stress management" became the buzz and stress became the ubiquitous diagnosis of the decade much like PTSD – post-traumatic stress syndrome or Bi-Polar disorder is today.

A plethora of books on the symptoms and physical and psychological consequences of stress populated bookstore shelves while at the same time corporate America became immersed in the wellness craze as a way to reduce healthcare costs and included stress management programs in wellness initiatives. I developed and delivered a number of these classes for mid to large-size to Fortune 500 companies during the time. The mantra most often spouted by corporate trainers, therapists and other mental health professionals in these classes was, "Stop and smell the roses."

This catchphrase which fast became a colloquialism has, in the last twenty plus years, been eclipsed by even greater demands and pressures that pull us every which way on the Doing Dimension. I've upgraded *Stress management* and *smelling the roses* in this millennium to *life balance* and *being present*. Whatever choice of words one uses and whenever the time frame, the challenge remains the same – being healthy and experiencing life fully, living deeply within one's core values. This is what the Being Dimension is all about.

Many people ask what they can do to be more present? Let's look at a few examples. Assume that your team is on a conference call at 7:00 AM. Being present means you're focused, attentive and able to override any distractions be they external, (your email inbox cries out for attention but you close the window down) or internal (thinking about the agenda for the next conference call but are able to bring your concentration back to the conversation at hand).

Consider when your our child is sharing his day, being present means you are *there*, fully attentive, focused on his every word and facial expression. By stepping off the Doing Dimension, you can enjoy being with him rather than thinking about grocery lists or telling him to be quiet while you pick up e-mails. Stop whatever you're doing, make eye contact and be singly focused -- be *there* "in the moment."

If we become addicted to busyness, the Doing Dimension becomes our master and seductively pulls us away from being present. We end up feeling overwhelmed, out of control, exhausted, resentful, and depressed.

The Doing Dimension is a fact of life – in fact it IS life. The more we can integrate the Being Dimension into the Doing Dimension, the more we become the masters of our lives. We end up feeling refreshed, centered, joyful and vibrant from moment to moment. In this day and age, juggling the balls is inevitable. The art of balance is being fully present while we're doing the juggling.

Doorways to Being

Focusing your attention, concentrating on the task or interaction is a challenge and requires persistence and patience. There are two tools or doorways that increase our ability to focus. The first is simple enough: just BREATHE mindfully. Yes, that's it. By focusing our awareness on our breath we will immediately find ourselves being more present, in the moment.

Like any other skill, practice is required. One exercise that helps is to use a counting sequence that is comfortable for you. So, for example, using the counting sequence of 5, 6, 8 you would do the following: Inhale on the count of five, 1-2-3-4-5, hold your breath on the count of six, 1-2-3-4-5-6, and then exhale on the count of eight, 1-2-3-4-5-6-7-8. Depending on where you are, you can either close your eyes or keep them open. As you breathe, think deeper, quieter, and slower with each and every breath.

Take just five minutes and do it right now. How does that feel? Even though your mental chatter may be going at high speed, pay attention to the spaces of silence between the noise. If you stay focused, you will experience moments of calm and peace. Be patient and aware. Periodically throughout this book, I'll remind you to stop and just breathe.

One time I was scheduled to do a seminar in Seattle and as I was boarding the plane, which was already delayed, I began to worry about whether or not I'd get there on time. As we were about to take off, the captain announced that there were some mechanical problems with our landing gear so we would have to wait on the tarmac until these were repaired. I freaked out! My mind went wild with thoughts of people sitting there looking at an empty podium. I had visions of the committee who hired me pacing around, furiously glaring at the clock. My thoughts further spun out as to how this would ruin my reputation, how I would never get another speaking engagement and on and on. Just then I remembered my own advice…Breathe. So, I did just that and I became present. I told myself there was nothing I could do about this situation so "just sit back and enjoy yourself right this minute." I have to admit, I did struggle back and forth between the mental noise and my breathing, but I was more *there* than I was not. And even though I was late for the event, the world didn't collapse. Someone delivered a "pinch hit" speech until I arrived.

Speaking of airports, I frequently overhear cell phone conversations while waiting to board. I've been struck by how often I hear at the end of the conversation, the usual perfunctory "I love you" said with as much meaning and presence as the "Hi. How are you?" we feel obliged to say to strangers. When I spoke to my son who lives in Syracuse, I found us guilty of the same glibness until I remembered to Breathe at which time I said with deep feeling, "You know, I really do love you." He was startled by the tone and said, "What's wrong with you? Are you sick or something?" Oh well. At least I was there.

At my seminars, I distribute 3x5 cards with the word BREATHE boldly printed on them. Attendees place these on their refrigerators, computers screens, auto visors or in their purses or wallets as a way to help them remember. I've received many positive comments about this little tool. "I keep my Breathe card on my desk and it not only reminds me to breathe -- it also reminds me to 'be present.' This is a great phrase that seems to come to mind at just the right times."

A Vice-President of a Fortune 500 company called me to tell me how helpful her Breathe card was. She said, "Well, I was multi-tasking and while on a conference call, I was picking up my e-mail at which time I realized that I forgot to send a very important memo out to my team in South America. I began to mentally spin out and there was an internal battle for my attention between the call and the unwritten memo. I happened to look up and saw the Breathe card on my desk and I can't tell you how it helped – I smiled to myself, moved my attention to my breath, did my usual counting sequence and I quickly felt a sense of calm at which time I was able to make a decision to focus on the call and do the memo as soon as I was able."

So no matter where you are, at the airport, on a conference call or with someone you love, the goal is to use your breath as a way to increase your presence, to experience balance while on the Doing Dimension. Remember, no one can live in a constant state of presence; only monks in ashrams can do that. The intent is simply to savor moments as we live our lives.

What's behind Doorway #2?

The second doorway involves spending time alone in silence either meditating or being in nature. Whenever I suggest sitting meditation to my clients, some moan and groan and say they just can't sit still or don't like being alone. "Ok," I say. "If you can't sit still then take yourself outside and be present…breathe mindfully in the midst of sky, sun, flowers, grass, insects, water, etc., etc."

As far back as 500 BC, Pythagoras suggested the following:

> *Learn to be silent.*
> *Let your*
> *Quiet mind*
> *Listen and absorb*

Solitude is essential to experiencing our natural state of balance. As we cultivate the ability to spend more time alone, the seed of this innate sense of balance grows and naturally begins to spill over into the Doing Dimension. Although I personally believe taking fifteen to twenty minutes a day to meditate – either sitting or walking -- is the most effective way to be with one's self, there are other avenues for solitude – any physical activity including gardening, knitting, receiving a massage, etc., where your mind is free to be.

I often see people jogging, walking or riding bikes with headphones on. This is exercise or recreation on the Doing Dimension. If we add the Being Dimension to the activity, there would be no headphones or other distractions -- just an awareness of our surroundings and our breath. Making time to do this increases our experience of balance and re-vitalizes us.

If we don't like being alone, we miss the opportunity to get re-acquainted with an old friend: ourselves. We can't know or like someone we don't spend time with.

Brain Sex

Men have an easier time when it comes to being focused – they're great at it.   Consider the intensity of their focus while golfing, jogging, or watching football on tv.   Nothing else in the universe exists. This talent comes with being able do only one thing at a time which, by the way, is biologically based. The corpus callosum, the cord that connects the left and right brain hemispheres, is on average 10% thinner than the average woman's and carries about 30% fewer connections between left and right. This is what gives men their one-thing-at-a-time approach to everything they do.

Whenever my husband and I are working on a project around the house, I'm spouting off what other projects we need to do next. He impatiently reminds me that he can only do one thing at a time. I'm exasperated by his inability to juggle and then I remember brain sex. This helps me realize that he's not being uncooperative or recalcitrant but that he is truly mentally capable of only doing one thing at a time. This awareness has reduced my nagging considerably thus putting less strain on our relationship.

The challenge for men in having a balanced life is being TOO focused – living in a zone of concentration that frequently excludes others' needs and feelings. The task becomes the master. This is what leads to life imbalance for them. Just as women are addicted to multi-tasks, men can be addicted to a single task – be it work, golf, exercise, etc. Either multi-tasking or single tasking can interfere with life balance – the Being Dimension is required for both. Stepping away from the task(s) and mindfully breathing or being in nature connects us to the miracle of our own being. This is what revitalizes us and gives us the motivation and energy to be productive.

Being comfortable with silence is another quality that men may have an easier time with. And again, this is the result of brain wiring. Women have specific speech and language areas located on both sides of the brain. Women are great talkers and since they store information differently than men do they *need* to talk. Male brains are highly compartmentalized so they have an innate ability to store and separate information which allows them to mentally put their problems on hold. Not so for women – we have to release our problems and aren't interested in finding solutions to them. In my marriage counseling sessions, I have found this to be one of the biggest issues couples struggle with. She says, "I just want him to talk more!" He says, "I don't know what she wants me to say. Whenever I offer a suggestion, she blows up!"

In their book, (which I highly recommend) *Why Men Don't Listen and Women Can't Read Maps*, (Broadway Books, 2000), Barbara and Allan Pease discuss these statistics: women speak, including body language gestures, on the average 20,000 communication "words" a day while men's daily average rounds out to about 7,000 communication "words." This has many implications but for the purposes of this book, this ability to be quiet and be singly focused (something we women have criticized men for) may be a real plus when it comes to life balance on the Being Dimension.

Recap

This chapter has suggested ways to live on the Being Dimension and is the heart of experiencing a balanced life.

Be aware
(Stop what you're doing)

Breathe
(Count 5, 6, 8)

Be Present
(Pay attention to the stillness within)

Breathe

Be in Nature

Breathe

Be Alone

Breathe

Two

❀

Being and Space

Whatever peace I know rests in the natural world in
feeling myself a part of it, even in a small way.

May Sarton

Did you ever notice how uncomfortable people are with silence?
We are quick to fill the space with chatter as if silence were something
to be dreaded. And what about the space of inactivity? Many high
achievers or Type A individuals experience significant anxiety if
they find themselves with nothing to do.

I have had a number of clients who fill the hour of our sessions
with incessant talking just so they don't have to really hear what
they're saying or feel what they're feeling. Remember Beth Ann?
I wondered if she had an oxygen tank strapped to her back because
she never seemed to come up for air!

I had to interrupt one client and tell her to stop talking and take
a two minute break. Within three seconds, she was chattering again.
Eventually, she learned that her inability to experience silence was
related to her unresolved sexual abuse. As long as she kept the
verbal and mental noise going, she wouldn't have to face the pain
and anger deep within.

People who live solely on the Doing Dimension overbook, over
schedule, double schedule, fill their time with one activity, one

meeting, one conversation after another. They cannot tolerate any space of time or inactivity dreading that it might stir up feelings of discomfort and fear. They believe that if they remain inactive, they might feel inadequate. Just *being* is often equated with laziness. Just *being* can tap into one's sense of worth – if someone feels good enough, he is more likely to be comfortable in silence or in solitude. Conversely, for people who do not, the space of nothingness taps into their own perceived sense of being nothing.

From our very first steps as infants, our sense of self-worth has been molded by the verbal and physical rewards we have received for our achievements and our productivity. One of my teen-age clients said, "My mom wants me involved in everything -- tennis, ballet, theatre, Student Government. She'll tell you that she puts no pressure on me and that I'm the one that wants to be involved in these things. But, you should see her beam when I'm performing. How can I not keep at it? I know this is really important to her. Sometimes I'd just like to be by myself but, whenever my mom catches me, she says, 'You're wasting time. Don't you have anything to do?'"

In the last five or so years, I've been struck by the number of activities kids are involved in. This not only adversely affects *their* sense of balance but clearly keeps parents spinning on the hamster wheel at warp speed.

Parents are frenetically chauffeuring their kids to every imaginable function during the week and on the week-ends. Not attending every activity be it soccer, baseball or ballet recitals creates intense waves of guilt and feelings of inadequacy for many parents.

Pat, a thirty-nine-year-old pharmaceutical sales rep, mother of four boys all of whom were either in select soccer, band, and/or music lessons, shared with her group at one of my seminars that her mother-in-law opened her eyes to how obsessive she was about attending these events and recitals.

"My husband and I would NEVER, EVER miss any of our boys' games or recitals. The guilt we experienced when we even *thought* about not going was too overwhelming. One day I had a particularly stressful time at work – I had to sell a new drug and I really wasn't as prepared as I should have been because two of my sons had activities the previous two nights which I attended, leaving me no time to prepare adequately. The doc's questions ended up keeping me at the office a lot longer than I expected. As I left I realized that I was going to be late for my oldest son's soccer game so I put the pedal to the metal and raced to the field, sprinted to the bleachers and sat down next to my mother-in-law completely out-of-breath. She looked over at me and said, 'Why do you feel like you have to attend every single game?' I was shocked! My mother-in-law was asking me this question?

"Because I want to be a good parent and I want Joey and the boys know that I'm interested and that I care. Didn't you go to *your* kids games? She looked at me and laughed. 'Actually, no I only went to the important ones and the lesser ones when I felt like it. As for showing your kids you care, don't you think you show that in a lot of other ways?' I was stunned and speechless. She went on to say, 'I think kids need to have some space from their parents so they can perform just for themselves.'

"At first I was miffed and silent but then as I thought about what she said I realized that she was absolutely right. Now, I ask the kids which games or recitals they would really like for us to attend. I can't tell you how that's helped me have more balance in my life."

As adults, we not only encourage our children to live their lives on hamster wheels but we are the hamsters, role modeling for them through our own frenetic schedules. If we're going to experience balance in our lives and teach our children to have balance, we must spend more time on the Being Dimension. We need to let our children see that living a balanced life is a priority for us. In addition to being role-models we also need to limit the number of activities they're involved in as well as monitoring TV time, computer time, game time.

The Power of Reflecting

If we're always on the go, when do we make the time to reflect, evaluate and assess our choices and decisions? During an interview, Marlon Brando was asked what his last words might be. He paused briefly and said, "What was THAT all about?" I hope my last words are, "I know exactly what my life was all about because I was *there* while it was happening."

For us to know what our lives are all about, we need to create space not only in order to be, but also to reflect, evaluate and assess how life is going, how our relationships are going, how our careers are going and so on. I'm not talking about navel gazing or obsessing. This is about taking, at the most, 10 minutes per day simply to review what's happening on the Doing Dimension of our lives. Once we've done that, we need to ask ourselves a few questions:

- Did this day reflect my personal values as they relate to my work ethic, self-care, my significant relationships, my spirituality?

- Were there moments of presence? Moments on the Being Dimension?

- What tough choices did I have to make in order to be more balanced today?

I do frequent keynote luncheon events with such organizations as Anthem Blue Cross Blue Shield, Spirit of Women and Jones of New York. Over the years I've been approached by a number of women who say that one of their colleagues was supposed to attend but backed out at the last minute because she had too much to do. "Too bad," they would say, "because this is exactly what she needed to hear."

Creating space means that we make the time for ourselves and for those activities, events and relationships that will enhance our experience of balance. No excuses. It means that we recognize the power of silence and are comfortable in its presence.

Making the Tough Choices

Often people seek counseling or attend personal growth seminars because they think the therapist or trainer has the magic bullet that has evaded them in their quest for balance or happiness. I have heard many people say during the course of my seminar, "I really know what I need to do to have a balanced life…Why can't I *do* it?"

Xiao Xing, a twenty-five-year-old single computer analyst sought counseling because she was unable to manage her weight. "I want an action plan!" She said emphatically. We came up with one and when she returned a few weeks later she hadn't followed through on any of her goals. When we explored this, she blurted out again, "I need an action plan!" "No," I said, "You need to make a commitment and look at the choices you're making." She sheepishly agreed and realized that wanting an action plan and executing it are two very different things.

In seeking to have balance, we have to make the tough choices – choices that may generate conflict with another person or intensify internal conflicts. If you keep doing the same old thing you keep getting the same old results.

Marissa, a forty-two-year-old advertising executive and her spouse, Jake, who is self-employed, recognized that their relationship was in trouble. With three kids, two dogs and a house on seven acres, they realized their attention for and to one another had been waning so they decided that they needed to commit to a "date" night once every other week. Within a month it became obvious to both how this time together gave their relationship a huge boost. "We actually discovered that we like each other!"

One day as she was leaving work to meet Jake for dinner, her ten–year-old daughter called in a frenzy. "She was hysterical. She wanted me to come home and help her with a project that she was having difficulty with. At first, I thought that Jake and I could skip our date night but then I realized I didn't want to miss our evening together. It was something that was very important to both of us. So, I told her to ask her older brother to help but her hysteria escalated. My mother guilt began to stab at my very heart and I found myself having this battle within – 'What kind of a mother are you?' 'What about Jake? Our relationship is important, too.'"

After asking her daughter a few more questions, Marissa assessed the situation and felt confident that her son could help. She made the decision to meet with Jake. "I have to tell you it was tough not going but after a glass of wine and some conversation with Jake, the guilt disappeared. And when I got home my daughter and son were laughing and eager to share what they had worked on together." I always tell my clients that guilt never killed anyone and it *always* passes. Don't let yourself be controlled by this overly-used emotion.

Knowing your core values (discussed in Chapter Five) and priorities, assessing the options and then making the tough choices one-day-at-a-time is what life balance is all about. And in order to make this happen, you have to step off the Doing Dimension and onto the Being Dimension to give you the space you need for reflection.

Recap

Be still.

Be silent.

Make the tough choices.

Three

———— ✿ ————

So How Much Do You Want to Change?

*Advice is what we ask for when we already
know the answer but wish we didn't.*

Erica Jong

Experiencing a balanced life requires a commitment on our part. Remember Xiao Xing? We all say we want a more balanced life, but actually few of us are willing to do *whatever it takes* to make it a reality.

"Who Me?"

Why are you reading this book? Have you attended one of my seminars? Did the title grab you? Are you sick and tired of being sick and tired? Whatever the reason, this book can change your life if you approach it with the mind set that you absolutely want to do something different to make your life better.

As a trainer and as a seminar participant myself, I realize there are motivational stages that people experience after reading a self-help book or attending a seminar. (This is assuming that the experience was meaningful!)

1st 24 hours	"It's a miracle!" People are buoyed by the experience and are inspired to change.
2nd 24 hours	"I'm making changes!" Some people are implementing behavior/attitude change.
3rd 24 hours	"Oh yeah, now what was I supposed to be doing?" Memory and motivation starts fading.
4th 24 hours	"What seminar??" It's totally gone.

This memory fade is natural – behavior change is never easy (although certainly not impossible) and we tend to resort to what's familiar and comfortable – the path of least resistance. Furthermore, a three to six hour seminar or a book is only the catalyst for behavior/ attitude change and is not actionable. I have grappled with the challenge of the "feel good" result vs. the actual behavior change result.

As a therapist, I confront clients who are not motivated enough to experience success encouraging them to come back when they are ready to change and, as a trainer, I do two things. First, the participants always complete a behaviorally based action plan and then they must choose an accountability partner to help keep them on track with their plan. Secondly, I challenge the organization who hires me to create reinforcement solutions. At one Fortune 500 company which was committed to life balance for its employees, we developed an internal website that was used as a self-directed learning site for ongoing re-inforcement of behavior change post-seminars.

Motivation of the Individual

From research done at the Brief Family Therapy Center in Milwaukee, Wisconsin, Steve de Shazer (1984, 1985, 1991) identified three types of clients who seek counseling. I've adapted this model and applied it to seminar participants. These types generally reflect the participants' desires and motivations to change behavior and take control of their lives.

Although this model can be used with any learning experience, I want you to apply it to yourself as a reader of this book. After all, your time is precious so why waste it on just reading? This isn't a pleasure book (although it will teach something that will bring you great pleasure). This book is about doing something. To realize its benefits you need to be committed to making behavior changes. So, which type of reader are you?

The Visitor

If you're a visitor, you basically read personal growth books or attend personal growth seminars because someone has asked you to -- possibly your boss or a friend who didn't want to go alone. You look at the experience as a time-filler or with skepticism. After all, you feel you're pretty smart and don't think anyone has much to offer you that you already don't know. Consequently, you see no reason to change your behavior.

You give a cursory eye to the material, sit back in judgment or toss the book aside with an attitude of "I knew that already." Or "I could've written that."

As a visitor, you may have to experience a crisis such as the dissolution of a relationship or a health problem before you become motivated to change your behavior.

The Complainant

As a complainant, you approach a book or seminar with enthusiasm as you recognize that your life is not where you want it to be. You know there is a problem but don't see your role in solving it or doing what's necessary to change things. You generally complain, make excuses and look outside yourself for a solution, pointing your finger at everyone else as the culprit in your unhappiness. "If only my partner would help out more." "If only my boss were more understanding." "If only the kids were more thoughtful," etc., etc. It's everyone else's fault. So, you read books to find ways to change the other people in your life.

You often feel like a victim and continually seek to control the outside world. As a victim you feel resentful and depressed much of the time.

The Customer

If you're a customer, you seek information and experiences that will give you the tools you need to change your behavior and improve your life. You are proactive and take responsibility for your role in the challenges you face and recognize that you're a part of the solution. Setting realistic behavioral goals, you are action-oriented and make no excuses for not achieving them. Synthesizing information, you sort out what works for you and then you make a plan to integrate your new learnings into your daily life. You're comfortable seeking out support. You're not afraid to ask for help because your relationships are reciprocal.

I like this perspective of Visitor, Complainant, and Customer because it can be used in any relationship or learning experience. It puts the responsibility where it belongs...within you.

Where Are You?

So, let's see where you are as you read this book or in your motivation to have a balanced life. On a scale of 1 to 10 with 1 being Visitor, 5 being Complainant and 10 being Customer, where do you fall in your willingness to make behavioral and attitudinal changes in order to experience a more balanced life?

Visitor				Complainant				I'll do what-ever it takes	
1	2	3	4	5	6	7	8	9	10

If it's anything less than an eight, put this book down until you get there.

Let's take a BREATHE (5-6-8) break. Close your eyes and focus your awareness on your breath. Pay attention to the rising and falling of your chest and look for the spaces of peace in between your mental chatter.

Recap

Generally, people read self-help books or attend personal growth seminars for three reasons:

1. As a time-filler or out of curiosity. (The Visitors who tends to deny they have any issues.)

2. As a way to fix everyone else in their lives. (The Complainants who tend to make excuses about why they can't make changes.)

3. As a way to improve quality of life and do whatever it takes to integrate the information/strategies into her daily life through behavior changes. (The Customers are proactive and take responsibility for their actions.)

Why is this important? The effectiveness of any intervention, be it therapy, a book or seminar or even a friend's advice, is directly related to the commitment level and sense of responsibility we are willing to take to solve our problems or improve our situations. I believe very strongly in the message of this book; consequently, I want you to benefit from it as much as possible. The only way for that to happen is for you to make a commitment to use the tools and strategies presented and to take responsibility for experiencing a balanced life. Something you deserve.

Four

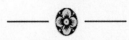

Valuing Yourself

I believe when all the dreams are dead, you're left only
with yourself. You'd better like yourself a lot.

Rita Mae Brown

One of the first things I ask women to do at my seminars is to find something in their purses that they value more than anything else. Stop and ask yourself right now, what your response would be. The usual items include pictures of children and grandchildren, pets. Once in a great while women will share pictures of their husbands but usually they were newlyweds! Some others pull out driver's licenses representative of independence or cell phones as something that keeps them connected to loved ones. Only one time did someone actually choose a mirror, which is the best answer and the one I'm after.

A mirror, you say? Yes, I do. A mirror because it reflects you -- and you need to value yourself more than anything else -- above kids, spouses, independence, etc. (Since we are created by a Higher Power, by valuing ourselves, we are valuing our spiritual nature. So to me, they are one and the same.) The usual reaction I get from many women is, "That seems so selfish!" Keep in mind that I am talking about being "self-centered or centered-in-your-self" not self-absorbed or selfish at the expense of others.

Women are notorious for putting everyone else first thus fostering unbalanced relationships. This often leads to resentments, anger and depression. There is a normal but frequently unexpressed need for reciprocity in our relationships. So, we keep on doing for others with the expectation that they will reciprocate – do for us. When that doesn't happen, we feel unappreciated, hurt and angry. When we become a priority to ourselves, we don't make any assumptions in our relationships. We know what we need, get it for ourselves or communicate clearly what it is we need from others. As a result, our expectations of others become much more realistic.

Sally, a thirty-eight-year-old married mother of three children ages 11, 9 and 7 sought counseling because she was feeling depressed. With a great husband, healthy and bright kids and a job she loved, she couldn't put her finger on why she was feeling so down in the dumps. About ½ way through the session, she started to weep. "I was so upset last week. It was my birthday and no one in my family remembered it. As the day wore on I kept waiting and thinking they're going to remember, they're going to remember. At 11:00 PM that night, I went into my room and cried. I couldn't believe it. I am so good to those kids and to my husband. I make birthdays a big deal in our family. I bake them their favorite cakes, take great care in choosing gifts they would really enjoy. How could they do this to me?" She wept even more. "What's even worse is that this isn't the first time. Just about every year, I keep hoping that this will be the year they'll remember. Oh well, it's just a birthday."

As we talked more, it became evident that Sally had many unspoken expectations for her family. The more they went unmet, the worse she felt.

I suggested that she share her feelings with her husband and kids directly and tell them what she expects when it comes to celebrating her birthday. She was astonished at the thought. "Well, if I told them, it wouldn't count then. They should just remember it and know what I'd like to have." I pointed out to her that her strategy wasn't working and that she needed to "coach" her family on what her needs were whether it be a birthday celebration, helping around the house or giving her some quiet time.

Through several months of therapy, Sally became more and more tuned in to her own needs and was able to assertively communicate them to friends and family. As a result, her relationships became more reciprocal and gratifying. As her birthday approached, she held a family meeting and made it clear what she expected. They had so much fun planning the celebration, they all decided to do this before everyone's birthday.

Let's take a BREATHE (5-6-8) break. Close your eyes and focus your awareness on your breath. Pay attention to the rising and falling of your chest and look for the spaces of peace in between your mental chatter.

Replenishing the Well

One would think that women, as nurturers of others, would be adept at nurturing themselves. Not so. When I speak to women about the importance of self-nurturing, I get many interesting responses. "I don't have time for that. I've got three kids and a full time job." "Self-nurture? I have no idea what I'd do to nurture myself." "I'll do that when the kids are gone." "I feel really guilty when I do anything for myself."

One of my favorite quotes comes from Mother Teresa. "To keep a lamp burning, you have to put oil in it." In order to have the energy and sense of well-being needed to juggle all our roles and responsibilities, it's absolutely essential that we make the time to self-nurture. The irony is that by not taking care of ourselves, our family and loved ones suffer greatly. Another of my favorite quotes – "When Mommy's happy everyone's happy." Every family should have this boldly displayed where it can be seen daily!

Although we find this irritating, men generally know exactly how to take care of themselves. Being "single-taskers," they are able to replenish themselves without letting other responsibilities creep into the equation.

Amelie, a twenty-eight-year-old married mother of two started her own business which was very successful but highly demanding. At one of the seminars, she shared her frustrations with her husband, Chad, at her table group.

"I get so mad at him I could split him in two – but then I think, who wants two of him!?" Amelie went on to say that usually Chad is very good with doing his share of the childcare and household chores but that over the last few months he had become lax and was golfing more often – like three times a week. "Normally I work-out on Thursday evenings and Saturday mornings while he stays with the kids but before I knew it his golf elbowed out my work-out time. On the day of my oldest son's birthday party, he was supposed to go grocery shopping. When I got home, the grocery bags were strewn all over the counter tops. I was furious! I knew he ran off to make his next tee time. When he got home I confronted him."

Chad responded quite vehemently that at least he went grocery shopping and he left out the things she needed for the party. Amelie laughed at that. "How would *you* know what I needed for the party?" He ignored her question and in no uncertain terms told her that he needed to golf because in the next three weeks his responsibilities at work would change and he wouldn't have as much time to play. "Besides, this new role I've been assigned to is going to be very stressful and golf really relaxes me."

Amelie went on to complain to the group that he didn't seem to care that she wasn't working out or getting her personal time needs met. "Even when I could sneak it into my schedule, I see the weeds so I have to do them or I see the dust bunnies hopping around. Is he blind??"

Sue, a member of the group told her that her perfectionism was getting in the way of her ability to take care of herself. "Chad," Sue said, "can see these things but he lets them go as he makes himself a priority when he needs to. Instead of blaming him, you need to come up with a creative solution like getting a babysitter on Thursdays and clearly telling him he has to be home on Saturday mornings."

With eyes downcast Amelie admitted that she has known she needed to be more proactive but that she just didn't have the energy. "It's easier to blame him."

So, Chad, like most men, is clear about what he needs to do for himself and does it. Good for him! Sometimes I think we women need to use men as role-models when it comes to self-care; we need to clearly and firmly communicate and negotiate what we need.

On the flip side, men need to balance their self-care with family needs and responsibilities. Joe, a thirty-year-old financial planner and father of two small children tells his stay-at-home wife Logan that he *has* to golf 18 holes *every* single Saturday and Sunday with his clients. On top of that he works 60 hour weeks. He came in to see me because his wife gave him a choice: "...go to counseling or get out because I'm not living like this anymore." "I don't understand it," he said truly perplexed. "I kill myself so she doesn't have to work and can stay at home with the kids and she just doesn't appreciate it."

After a few sessions, Joe admitted that he was a golf addict and justified his week-end absences from home as work-related. "My boss has told me many times to go home at night but I liked staying at work rather than dealing with Logan." Just like women who make excuses when it comes to making time for themselves, similarly men can do the same when it comes to pitching in with childcare and/or household responsibilities.

The Guilt Factor

This idea of self-nurturing presents women with a special challenge – dealing with guilt. Due to socialization, women experience much higher levels of guilt. For most men, guilt quickly washes over them as they move into problem solution mode. For us women, guilt seems to hang around like a London fog.

Doing something pleasurable and relaxing just for ourselves can be disquieting particularly when guilt feelings surface and this little voice in our heads whispers, "How can you sit here and read? You have so much to do. Get up off your lazy butt and get going." "This isn't right having a massage. This money should be going toward the kids' athletic fees." "What kind of mother are you? Sitting here while your kids are making dinner?" What are some of the voices in your head?

I think we women spend too much time swimming around in guilt – mother guilt, daughter guilt, work guilt, friend guilt, etc., etc., etc. We give in to it far too often and this capitulation only gives it more power over us. Men seem to be able to be more self-forgiving and less critical than we are. In other words, they don't personalize criticisms or conflicts. Now I realize there is a disparity in the cultural standards for men and women as well as biological differences which go beyond the scope of this book. Suffice it to say that we could learn a few things from men on this one.

Guilt is an emotion experienced after doing something wrong. The behavior that activates guilt violates a moral or ethical code. Generally people experience guilt when they have broken a rule or in some way violated their own beliefs or standards.

There are two types of guilt: healthy guilt and toxic guilt. Healthy guilt keeps us connected to our sense of right and wrong and to our personal values. If we believe missing church on Sunday is wrong, we'll experience guilt when we do. If we believe cheating on our income tax is wrong, we'll feel guilty if we do.

Toxic guilt keeps us trapped in someone else's standards and values. It's an automatic reaction to something we're doing – a reaction which we generally don't question or re-evaluate for ourselves. Guilt is related to the standards we set for ourselves – if these standards are perfectionistic or rigid, guilt will become a ghost forever haunting us. We need to determine what's at the root of our guilt feelings. Toxic guilt obfuscates our ability to find solutions to the guilt trigger and keeps us in a state of self-doubt and self-recrimination.

Sue Ellen, a forty-nine-year-old single divorcee, came to see me because she was feeling deeply guilty about her decision to take a cruise. "I really shouldn't spend the money. It's frivolous and I'll have nothing to show for it when I'm done. But I'd so love to go. You know, I've never been able to spend money on myself. The guilt is suffocating."

I asked, "Where do you get the idea that you shouldn't spend money on yourself?"

"When I was growing up, anytime I wanted anything for myself, like a doll or when I got older and wanted make-up, my mother, who never spent a dime on herself, would reprimand me for being selfish and a spendthrift. As a young child, she did go through the Depression." She went on with a tinge of pride in her voice, "That woman could rub two nickels together and make a dollar."

As we talked, I challenged Sue Ellen to re-evaluate her mother's values related to spending and how they no longer applied in her life. "Well, you're right," she said. "I'm an attorney and I make very good money. Thanks to my mom, I've saved most of it. But I sure haven't had much fun while I was pinching those pennies!"

"Well," I said, "isn't it time you started to enjoy the fruits of your labor without punishing yourself for it with guilt? Not spending on yourself was your mother's value and it was based on her early childhood experiences. Whenever you hear that little voice, I want you to neutralize it by countering it with, 'I deserve to take this cruise. I don't have to be trapped by my mom's admonitions anymore.'"

What are we doing wrong when we take time to self-nurture, to experience something enjoyable and relaxing for ourselves? If we feel guilty while we're self-nurturing, we need to reflect on what standard we've violated? Is it truly ours? Is it society's? Is it our mother's? Whose?

It's understandable if we feel guilty for making tough choices like Marissa did with her husband, Jake, in lieu of helping her daughter. The difference is that if the choice is aligned with our values, the guilt hits with a "ping" and not with the force of cannonball.

If we keep giving in to that little guilt-inducing voice, we'll never be able to fully savor the joy of being alive. So, we need simply to ignore those messages and neutralize them by saying to ourselves, "Nurturing myself is another way to nurture my family and loved ones." And by the way, no one I know of died from an overdose of self-inflicted guilt! They were just miserable. So, stand up to the toxic guilt as every time you do, you weaken its strength.

Let's take a BREATHE (5-6-8) break. Close your eyes and focus your awareness on your breath. Pay attention to the rising and falling of your chest and look for the spaces of peace in between your mental chatter.

The Ripple Effect

In addition to my clinical work with adults, I have also treated adolescents and their families. Through this work, I have realized how important it is for moms to meet their own needs and to be able to self-nurture because they set the emotional climate for the family. A mother's overall tone and energy is felt by the entire family – especially by the kids. And if she is feeling stretched, unappreciated and out-of-control, kids will act out this unhappiness.

Whenever moms bring their kids in for counseling (dads generally leave this responsibility to their partners) their initial motivation is to "fix" the teen. After meeting with the youngster, I always follow up with mom to determine the quality of her life, i.e., relationships, ability to self-nurture, etc. Usually, mom is in the stressed-to-the-max mode and is totally neglecting herself. Once I have a few sessions with mom and work with her on taking better care of herself, the youngster's behavior improves. Don't ever forget, "When Mommy's happy, everyone's happy."

When Bev, a forty-year-old married mother of one daughter, walked into my office she was talking before she even sat down on the couch. "My daughter Rebecca who's 16 seems to be somewhat depressed. She's been a B+ student but lately she's been getting D's and F's. She's holed up in her room which by the way is a complete pigsty and she's constantly arguing with her dad and me. She's driving us crazy."

Bev's husband didn't feel the need to meet with me and neither did Rebecca (at first), so Bev and I worked on her relationship with her daughter, which seemed to be deteriorating. Throughout our sessions, it became clear to me that Bev was overly involved in her daughter's life. She expressed great concern about Rebecca leaving for college in the fall and wondered if she was ready to take the leap.

I asked Bev if she would ask Rebecca once again if she would be willing to meet with me alone in order to help me understand the situation better. Surprisingly, she finally agreed.

"Ok Rebecca," I said, "I know you don't want to be here which I can understand and actually, I'd rather you not be here either. You know, you should be hanging out with friends or on the phone…"

She interrupted me, "Or at La Crosse practice."

"Ok, so what's the deal with your mom? She's worried about you."

"You know, my mom needs to get a life. Even though she works, that's all she does. She really has no friends and she's in my face all the time."

"I'll make a deal with you," I said, "If I help your mom get a life, would you be a bit more cooperative at home? You know, get those grades up, clean up your room and adjust that attitude of yours?"

"Maybe," and with that we ended our session.

The next time I met with Bev, I focused more on her, which was a challenge since she had a difficult time talking about herself. "You know Bev, I'd like to get to know you a little better." She squirmed a bit. "Tell me about you…your interests, what you like to do for fun…"

"Interests? I work – who has time for hobbies? And anyway, I have no idea what my interests are. Rebecca loves La Crosse…I go to every single game. As for fun…I've always had fun with Rebecca before she became a teenager!"

"What are you going to do when she leaves for college next year?"

She was silent for the longest time and then when she spoke her voice cracked with emotion, "I really don't know. My life will be so empty without her."

For the next few sessions, Bev and I worked on helping her establish a life without Rebecca. We discussed possible interests and she had many, although she had never pursued any of them. When we talked about her marriage, she said, "You know, I don't even know my husband anymore. We haven't done anything together, I guess, since Rebecca's been born."

Over the course of therapy, Bev took up painting, developed some friends from her art class, and went on a few week-end trips with her husband. I saw her change from an anxiety ridden woman to someone who laughed and seemed to enjoy her life.

At one of our last sessions she said, "I don't know how this has happened but Rebecca has been a changed child. She seems happier, her grades are better, not perfect, but better and I don't have to tell her to clean her room! She's a delight to be with -- well, most of the time!" she winked.

"As for George, things are better in that department as well. He's laughing at my jokes and we're taking evening walks. It's a miracle!"

The miracle was that Bev began taking care of herself and meeting her own needs. It rippled out to Rebecca and George. I've never seen this fail.

Let's take a BREATHE (5-6-8) break. Close your eyes and focus your awareness on your breath. Pay attention to the rising and falling of your chest and look for the spaces of peace in between your mental chatter.

Mindless Self-Nurturing

When self-nurturing comes up in my conversations with women, some will say, "Not a problem for me. I get massages, have my nails done, etc." That's great, I say. But are you there when you're having the massage or are you thinking about work or what you have to do when you get home? If your mind is elsewhere while you're self-nurturing, you're on the Doing Dimension – it does not count!

Self-nurturing activities must spring from the Being Dimension where we are fully aware and present during the experience. So whether we're walking, having a massage, taking a bubble bath, or singing -- whatever replenishes us, it can only be of benefit when we're there.

Recap

One way to value ourselves is by cultivating reciprocal relationships and by nurturing ourselves.

- Self-nurturing is essential to our health and well-being as well as to the important people in our lives. The world will be a better place if we all nurtured ourselves and replenished our spirits.

- There shall be no guilt while self-nurturing and there won't be if we recognize the difference between healthy guilt and toxic guilt. Toxic guilt is experienced when we live our lives according to someone else's standards and/or value system or if we have perfectionistic standards for ourselves.

- Self-nurturing must spring from the Being Dimension where we are fully aware and present during the experience. It will only be of benefit when we are fully there.

Five

— ❀ —

Reconciling Our Vision

Sometimes I think I think I understand everything
and then I regain consciousness.

Anonymous

Throughout my developing years, I would envision what my life would be like when I became an adult. So, when I was in my teens, I envisioned that I would be married by age twenty-five to a great and successful guy and start a family. I had this mental movie as to exactly how my life would go and I could see everything from the kind of house I would have to how I would be a wonderful teacher, a career that would allow me to be home for my kids, how I'd be a terrific mom who was a great cook and housekeeper who would always be there for my family no matter what. And last but not least, I saw myself as a totally devoted partner and mother.

In creating this vision, I used my mother as a role-model. In my mind, she was the perfect woman – great cook, efficient household manager, good listener, adoring wife, loving sister and very attentive mother. Whether we realize it or not, we use our moms as role-models regardless of how good or not-so-good we thought they were. (On the not-so-good side, we consciously choose to be the opposite of what we didn't appreciate or like about her.)

Well, as fate would have it, my mental movie was no match for the reality my life became. At twenty five-years-old, I was a divorced single mom with no financial support from my ex. I had to live with my parents and was working and going to school 24/7. Needless to say, I had to alter my vision. And although I altered the obvious, it took me years to realize that I clung to the underlying perfectionism of how I was going to be as a person, a mother, an employee, etc. Check out the adjectives I used in my visioning process...a "wonderful teacher," a "terrific mom," who would "always" be there and a "totally devoted partner and mother." This was reinforced by that image of my mom in my head. Throughout my twenties and thirties, I continually measured myself against these standards, and this continually generated feelings of inadequacy and depression.

Interestingly enough, through my graduate studies and my clinical work, I discovered two things that helped me adjust my expectations. The first was that my mom didn't work outside the home! I forgot about that small detail when I kept comparing myself to her and always fell short. The second was that I was not alone. Most women have life visions and many of them were also plagued with what I call PSS -- the Perfectionistic Standards Syndrome that I'll discuss later in this chapter.

Prior to the early to mid 1990s, women typically described their life visions in terms of events – when I get married, when I have my first baby, when my child starts school, when my partner or I get a promotion, when we buy our first house, etc. As life balance has increasingly become an issue for women, their life visions focused more on having a balanced life – being able to juggle all the balls without dropping a one.

Even though the central theme of life visioning for women shifted to achieving balance, perfectionistic standards continued to permeate the picture.

How Am I Doing?

Given our culture's proclivity for competitiveness, we all want to know how we compare – whether it's to others or to our own standards. Our life vision can be a source of satisfaction to us or a source of great unhappiness depending upon the disparity between our life vision and our *real* life situation. If we're suffering from PSS – Perfectionistic Standards Syndrome – our life vision will drive us to despair.

I ask you first take out a piece of paper and write down your life balance vision. What does life balance mean to you?

The next step is to reflect on how this vision compares to your real life. How realistic is this vision given your *current* life situation and stage of life? What are you expecting from yourself? What are you expecting from others in your life? Now that's where the perfectionism comes in. Do you want to be all things to all people? Do you think that asking for help or support is a weakness? Are there a lot of "shoulds" in your vision? For example, "I *should* be more organized," "I *should* make more time for the kids, partner, whomever." "I *shouldn't* yell at the kids." "I *should* be able to do it all without help."

If you've answered "yes" to many of these questions and those "*should*" statements sound familiar, you need to alter your life balance vision to one that is realistic -- one that allows you to be a human being. This is the first step in our journey toward experiencing a balanced life.

Perfect Pattys

Let me give you some real examples of PSS starting with a few of the responses I've received from the work/life balance seminars I've conducted. Here's an anonymous response to the work/life balance vision question.

"For me work/life balance is achieved when I am able to merge the two and can flow effortlessly between the two without feelings of guilt...If I have achieved work/life balance I'll feel satisfied as a whole person rather than satisfied with just one part of my life."

Flowing "effortlessly" between work and family sounds unrealistic and pretty perfectionistic to me! Throw in "without feelings of guilt" and "satisfied as a whole person" and you've got a vision that can only perpetuate feelings of inadequacy.

Here's another one from Klio, a thirty-eight-year-old manager, single mother of three.

"Achieving work/life balance means having the time to enjoy my family and get all of my work done and still have time to invest in myself"

This is a simple one but it's loaded with idealism and perfectionism. When I asked Klio if she thought she could ever achieve this, her eyes welled up with tears and she said, "I could if only I were more organized and self-disciplined. It's hard to enjoy my family when I seem to be yelling at them all of the time. I have no patience." I took it a step further and asked her what she would do if she had time to invest in herself to which she deeply sighed and said, "I don't really know. I never think about that. I have three kids to raise."

Keep in mind, the more idealistic your vision is and the farther it is from the reality of your current life situation, the unhappier you will be with yourself and your life.

I worked with Klio to re-define her vision and this is what she came up with,

Balance means being able to establish daily priorities each morning, raising my awareness to the opportunites to be assertive at work and at home, and taking at least 10 minutes a day for myself to decompress.

Knowing what I know of her, this vision is much more realistic and practical and if she is a "Customer," she will undoubtedly improve her sense of well-being.

Let's take a BREATHE (5-6-8) break. Close your eyes and focus your awareness on your breath. Pay attention to the rising and falling of your chest and look for the spaces of peace in between your mental chatter.

Dyan's Melt Down

One client whom I saw is another illustration of the point I'm trying to make. Dyan, a 45-year-old mother of four children ages 15, 13, 10, and 2 was a full-time nurse and married for the 2nd time. The youngest child was born of the 2nd marriage. When I asked Dyan what prompted her to seek counseling, she sobbed and said, "I'm a failure -- a total failure. Last Saturday, I had a major melt down which is so unlike me. I screamed at my husband, threw dishes at him and told the kids I was going to pack up and leave all of them."

As our session continued, Dyan filled in the details of that fateful day. The night before, she had worked a late shift at the hospital and got up early that day since her husband had invited his staff over for a cook-out. There was much to do: grocery shopping, cooking, cleaning, driving the 10 year old to her soccer game and, of course, there was the never ending laundry to do. Upon returning from grocery shopping, she noticed that the grass needed to be cut so she hurried inside to put the groceries away. While doing so, two of the kids broke into fisticuffs over a video game and as she was running over to referee, her husband, who was sitting on the couch watching golf, said to her, "Hey, could give me a neck-rub? I had a really bad day."

"That's when I went berserk," she said. "I just snapped. I couldn't handle it. I can't figure out what's wrong with me. I shouldn't have reacted that way, after all, he just wanted a neck rub."

Dyan blamed herself for her reaction rather than assessing the situation for what triggered it and what she could do differently to prevent it from happening again. As we continued to talk, Dyan mentioned "the Brady Bunch" several times. "I wanted us to be like the Brady Bunch." Upon further exploration, Dyan's vision for a balanced life was this TV family. I looked at her and said, "You mean you're comparing yourself to Carol Brady who didn't work and had a full time maid?"

At that point she laughed and realized how ridiculous this was. Many women I've worked with have these unrealistic life balance visions floating around in their heads and most of them have never verbalized them to anyone. Consequently, they're evaluating their lives based on some unspoken and unexplored life balance vision that is often shaped and influenced by their mothers or major caretakers, aunts, teachers or mentors. And most likely, none of these women have had the same identical life challenges and choices.

Men have their own oft unspoken visions of life balance. The influence of their parents/dad, the culture, media, peers, etc., presents them with a set of self-imposed standards and comparison points. I facilitate one exercise that helps both men and women examine their own socialization by doing an exercise. They are to identify the adult caretakers in their family of origin. So, it could be a mom, dad, a step-parent, a grandparent or gay partners. On a sheet of paper they are to draw four columns (for purposes of example I'm using a traditional family) labeled as:

My mom as mom	My mom as partner/spouse	My dad as dad	My dad as partner/spouse

They then brainstorm and list all of the responsibilities they remember each adult caretaker doing within the family. Next they are to review these and circle the ones that their partner is doing and then circle those that they are doing. This has been very eye opening for many of them as they are able to actually see the division of labor they grew up with and determine if they are continuing the same patterns.

This exercise helps people re-establish balance visions related to their family that are more realistic given their current life situations.

So I'm asking you to share your work/life balance vision with someone you trust and get some honest feedback. In the work/life balance seminars I conduct, sharing in small groups is the most powerful, life-changing aspect of the entire experience. Life is so busy; we don't make the time to connect with other people to do some work/life balance reality testing.

And as for Dyan, one of her major issues was realizing that she needed to ask for help, be assertive and negotiate household responsibilities with her husband and the older kids. This same characteristic spilled over into work and in all of her other relationships. Suffering from PSS, she saw asking for help as a weakness. I told her more melt downs were on their way unless she found Carol Brady's maid, Alice, to pitch in and help her. That's when she said, "All right, I get it. Can I bring my husband to the next appointment?" She did and after many months of intensive marriage therapy, she decided that the relationship wasn't a viable one for her. He continued to be uninvolved in the family and household responsibilities. Dyan and her husband separated and eventually divorced. At our last session Dyan said that this was the most difficult decision of her life but she went on to say, "I knew I was expecting him to be someone he wasn't. Although I'm feeling a great deal of sadness, I'm also feeling a tremendous amount of relief. I know the kids and I will be just fine."

Core Values

Once you have identified and refined your vision, the next step is to crystallize your core values as they are the driving force behind the decisions you make regarding life balance. Many people live according to a set of values but oftentimes do so unconsciously. Living your life in this way is like taking a journey without a map and hoping you arrive at your destination somehow. Not having clearly established core values can lead to feelings of anxiety, uncertainty and trance-like living.

Remember Klio's vision ? *Balance means being able to establish daily priorities each morning, raising my awareness to the opportunites to be assertive at work and at home, and taking at least 10 minutes a day for myself to decompress.* The next step for her is to identify her core values so she will be better able to prioritize. If she does not include her self-care as a core value or know her other core values, she is much less likely to realize her vision.

In Chapter Two I talked about Marissa who had to make the tough choice between having dinner with her spouse and helping her daughter on a school project. Although having strong family relationships and being available to family members was one of Marissa's core values, she had to assess the situation to determine whether she was going to be available to her daughter or strengthen her relationship with her husband, Jake. Rather than trying to do both which would have created a great deal of stress for her and most likely irritation for her daughter and spouse because she would have been distracted being pulled in two directions, she made a tough choice to be with Jake so that she could be fully available and present while with him.

In having life balance, we must realize that we simply can not do it all – we have to make tough choices and in order to do that we must know what our core values/priorities are. I give you an opportunity to crystallize your core values in the next chapter.

People who suffer from PSS (Perfectionistic Standards Syndrome) have a particular challenge in accepting the idea that tough choices have to be made in living a balanced life one-day-at-a-time. Their mindset clings to the notion that they "should" be able to do it all and they desperately try to do so. Letting go of these unrealistic expectations/standards, shifting away from all-or-none thinking and looking for the gray areas that encompass every choice is the clearest path to a balanced life.

Recap

Reconciling our life visions is a critical step in having a balanced life.

- Write down your work/life balance vision and be sure to include your core values

- Share it with someone you respect or a group

- Assess its viability given your current life situation

- Check for unrealistic/perfectionistic standards or expectations

Six

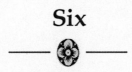

Determing Resources

*Getting what you go after is success, but liking
it while you are getting it is happiness.*

Bertha Damon

Let's look at what comprises our visions, our core values and our lives. Although each individual has a unique life situation, four areas that people have to contend with on a daily basis can be identified: Work, Family, Support System, and Personal Care. I find having a conceptual framework is highly useful in thinking about life balance.

I, along with my colleague, Maria Aracocha White, elaborated on each of these elements and refer to them as the Four Quadrant Life Balance Model located on the next page. We view each of the quadrants as consisting of a series of resources that comprise a balanced life. As you look at the model, review each quadrant and see how you fare at this point in time.

Are the descriptors in each quadrant a resource or a liability for you? For example, in the Work Resource Quadrant, do you take advantage of your company's benefits or are you afraid to because it would adversely affect your career? If you use your benefits, they are a resource; if you don't, they become a liability in your balance equation. If any of the resources in each of the quadrants becomes a liability, your sense of balance will destabilize. The more liabilities, the greater the destabilization will be.

FOUR QUADRANT WORK/LIFE BALANCE MODEL

Work Resources	Family Resources

Educational opportunities
Manageable Travel
Available benefits
Career advancement opportunities
Challenging/meaningful work
Regular work hours
Autonomy
Flexibility
Mentor/Coach
Sense of being valued
	Physically and emotionally healthy
	   family members (nuclear and
	   extended)
	Positive, supportive & available
	   partner
	Supportive extended family
	Financial security

Support Resources	**Personal Care Resources**

Network of supportive and available
   female friends
Good and sufficient childcare/
   household help
Adequate financial resources
Ability to <u>ask</u> for help/support
Confidante or two
	Making time for yourself
	Being physically & nutritionally fit
	Setting clear boundaries with others
	Knowing out-of-balance symptoms
	Creating space for reflection
	Having a spiritual side
	Having a sense of humor
	Maintaining an optimistic attitude
	Effectively managing emotions

Work Life

Companies often offer employees benefits that promote work/life balance such as job sharing, flextime, maternity benefits or family leave time. Yet, many people I've talked to either don't know what their benefits are or hesitate to utilize them fearing the impact on their career path. One of my seminar participants said, "If you're worried that your career will be affected by asking for what you need, you're working at the wrong company."

Liz, a forty-two-year-old married mother of two, came to see me because she was very unhappy in her current job. Since she had been in this assignment, she found her manager to be demanding, rigid and insensitive to working mothers. He frequently expected his team to work the same 60-70 hour week he did. She was reluctant to challenge his expectations for fear it would create greater tension between the two of them or, even worse, result in the loss of her job. She had been with the company for over 15 years and had planned to retire there. To make matters worse, she was the major breadwinner in the family.

When I met with Liz she was at the breaking point. "My family is suffering because I'm never home and when I am home I'm uptight worrying about what I have to do at work. I've developed ulcers and I'm on Prilosec. This is no life." After many sleepless nights and numerous conversations with her husband, Liz decided she had to do something. "Joe and I decided that if we have to sell the house and readjust our lifestyle, we would do it. So imagining the worst, I met with the VP last week and told him I could no longer continue in this assignment because it was affecting my health and my family. To my great surprise AND relief he was incredibly supportive! We discussed what my options were as well as a time frame for the transition into another assignment. His only request was that I meet with my boss and discuss this with him which I did yesterday. And that went surprisingly well. I can't tell you how empowered I feel."

We often have to take risks and make tough decisions in order to have a more balanced life. Having clarity about our values and priorities helps us along the way. Liz was willing to risk her job and make significant lifestyle changes for what was even more important to her – her health and her family.

Steve, a forty-three-year-old marketing executive, realized that he needed to re-evaluate his work schedule after his wife left him. "It seems I wasn't getting the message but when she left, I got it loud and clear. I realized that my number one priority should have been my family." His 70 hour work weeks were wreaking havoc on the family which included four children. "I was volatile and becoming increasingly hostile and irritable at home with everyone – I wasn't aware just how miserable I was." After meeting with his boss to re-negotiate some of his responsibilities and corporate expectations, Steve decided it was time to look for another job in an organization with a culture that was in greater alignment with his personal values.

Take a look at the Work Resources Quadrant and circle those items that are important to you. Does your work life reflect what you've circled? If not, it's time to assess your company's culture to see if it's in alignment with your values. If it is, then the next step is to meet with your boss and begin the process of negotiating your work life needs, whether it's hours, travel time, career advancement, or something else. If that fails, you may have to decide, as Steve did, if this organization is an appropriate fit for you at this point in your life.

Family Life

At my keynotes I frequently ask the audience what they think women complain about the most and inevitably the most common response is "spouses." Once the laughter subsides, I share with them just how important spouses/partners are to having a balanced life. Based on research done at Stanford University and my own clinical experience, women cite having a supportive and positive partner as *the* most critical factor in being able to balance their lives. I believe that men need the same kind of support. The difference is that most men get it because women have been socialized to provide it. Many men, on the other hand, need to be coached and directed when it comes to household/childcare support and involvement. Oftentimes women resent this and expect that their partners should just see what needs to be done and do it.

Back to brain sex. According to Barbara and Alan Pease (2000), "Women are equipped with far more finely tuned sensory skills than men and have an acute ability to notice small details, and changes in appearance or in the behavior of others." They go on to say that research at the University of Pennsylvania used brain scan tests to show that when a man's brain is in a resting state, at least 70% of its electrical activity is shut down. Scans of women's brains showed 90% activity during the same state. This confirms that women's brains are wired to constantly receive and analyze information from their environment. From a more practical standpoint, women have wider peripheral vision than men so they just plain see more! Men, on the other hand, literally have tunnel vision. This goes back to primitive times – they needed long distance tunnel vision that would allow them to be better at hunting.

When I point this out to my clients or ask them to read *Why Men Don't Listen and Women Can't Read Maps* (Broadway Books, 2000), they're more willing to change their expectations and provide more coaching to their partners. Changing this mindset is most difficult because we like to think that if our partners really loved us and/or the kids they would be more involved. Very dangerous thinking!

Much of the anxiety and depression women share in my office is related to having a partner who is negative or non-supportive in parenting and who only minimally contributes to the household responsibilities. Having a partner who isn't supportive and understanding is a major factor to feeling out of balance.

At one of my follow-up sessions, Joan, a thirty-eight-year-old mother of six, proudly shared that when Dan, her ten-year-old son, needed an emergency dental visit, she called her husband and told him he'd have to leave work and take Dan because she had a critical deadline to meet by day's end. Her husband said he couldn't due to very important meetings which he had that day. "You know," Joan said to the group, "I *knew* that was an excuse because just the day before he told me he had a very light week!" So I just told him in no uncertain terms, "Well, then I'm going to have to call your boss and see if those meetings are more important than your son." Needless to say, her husband took Dan to the dentist.

Some women simply accept what a spouse or partner says he can and cannot do when it comes to family/household responsibilities while boiling with anger on the inside. This is the result of an inability to assert themselves appropriately. Other women – and men, too – suffer from the proverbial martyr complex. Rather than have a more reciprocal relationship, they take pride in their hyper-tasking and allow partners to do nothing so they can feel indispensable and needed. They hold their significant others emotionally hostage by constantly reminding them just how much they do. Underneath this behavior pattern is someone who needs control and is fear-based, only seeing her love-ability in terms of what she DOES for others.

Whether it's a communication deficit or a need to be in control, the ripple effect from having a non-supportive partner/spouse often results in a great deal of resentment and anger for both and this can lead to dysfunctional communication patterns. Accusations, deadly silences and defensive reactions become more and more frequent. So what's the solution?

Margaret, a thirty-nine-year-old lesbian, mother of two, sought counseling because of the increasing rage she was experiencing toward her partner of 11 years. Her greatest complaint was that this was not a reciprocal relationship and that her partner, Sherry seemed to control everything and everyone. "I do everything around here. And what really upsets me is that whatever I do is never good enough for her. So, we get into these huge fights. They're brutal." Over the course of therapy, Margaret kept complaining about Sherry and when I suggested that one of her options was to end the relationship, she welled up with tears and said in a whisper, "But, I love her."

"Your complaining and fighting isn't working. So your only other option is to accept Sherry for the perfectionist she is."

"Accept her as she is?" she asked with a grimace.

"The truth hurts but the truth will set you free."

We both laughed. I went on, "You can't just love the good parts of someone. Let's work on you being able to tolerate her criticism without personalizing it. Tell her that if she doesn't like how you do something, she can always do it herself. Once you're able to communicate in a calm, non-defensive and assertive manner, I'll bet the fights won't get so out of hand and Sherry will get the message."

"Well, I've always felt I had to do it her way."

"That's the problem. Rather than react, respond to her calmly. Sometimes you might even ignore her criticisms. Detach… detach…detach. I mean that in a healthy way. If you accept her as a perfectionist, you'll be much less likely to personalize her criticisms and get defensive."

Over the course of several months, Margaret worked on her communication style. She was able to emotionally detach from Sherry's criticism. Their fights diminished considerably and their relationship improved.

The solution to a non-supportive relationship is to first understand that there are biological gender differences in processing and analyzing information from the environment and then to either truly accept your partner/spouse for who s/he is, work on negotiation/ assertiveness skills or, if the relationship continues to be a nonviable one, end it. Life is too short.

Balance and the Single Woman

I realize not everyone is married or in committed partnerships. So what about single folks? Many single people feel that work/life balance seminars and books solely focus on partnered individuals with families and rightfully so. They are a neglected group. Although employees with children have additional stresses, single people without children have their own challenges when it comes to the balancing act.

Frequently given extra assignments, expected to work longer hours or travel excessively because they don't have a "family," single people are left wondering how they are *ever* going to have a relationship if they're never available to go out and meet people!

Malti, a twenty-nine-year-old IT manager, sought counseling because she was becoming increasingly negative and depressed. "I don't know what's wrong with me. I feel like I'm in a dark cave perseverating on how miserable I am." As we talked, Malti shared that she feels very isolated both at work and in her personal life. "Everyone talks about their partners or kids at work. Nobody thinks to ask me about my family or my life. It seems like almost all company social events require a mate or a date." Tears slipped down her cheeks. "When an assignment comes up that requires travel, my boss immediately looks to me to fill it because I'm the only single person on the management team. I just feel less valued as a person and more of a workhorse because I'm single." Malti knew she had to push back but she was afraid she would be perceived as someone who was not willing to be a team player.

I asked her if she was able to assertively share her life with the group. "When they start showing pictures of kids or partners, show pictures of those two dogs you love so much. And don't forget your nieces and nephews. Just because they don't ask doesn't mean you can't tell!"

It was clear that she also needed to meet with her boss – a forty-five-year-old married man with three children – and educate him on the requirements of being a successful single working person within the organization. We came up with four areas that she wanted to discuss: work/travel expectations, more personal development training, a mentor and diversity as it relates to being single. "My company is very committed to diversity and I think the big wigs at the top forgot that single people have their own unique needs and lifestyle issues."

Several weeks later at one of our sessions, Malti shared that things were slowly getting better. She reported that initially the meeting with her boss was a little awkward as he became defensive but she remained calm and firm and within a few minutes his demeanor relaxed. After some discussion, he conceded that he needed to work with the team to develop a more equitable travel and emergency rotation schedule.

"I feel like there's a light at the end of the tunnel now." She giggled. "By the way, when we have the next 'Kids at Work Day', I've already informed everyone I'm bringing my dogs!!"

Tough choices continue to be a lynchpin to having a balanced life. If, after discussing the diverse needs of being single with a boss there is no change, it's time to get the resume out.

Petra, a thirty-year-old department head, decided to seek counseling because she was having very ambivalent feelings about whether or not she should look for another job. She was feeling very frustrated with the amount of additional responsibilities she was having to assume because two of her team members took a significant amount of time off for childcare issues. That, coupled with being assigned emergency projects over week-ends became too much to deal with.

"I have eight years vested in this company and I really don't want to leave. I'm considered to be a 'fast tracker' and I know I have much to offer but I want a life! I've talked to my boss but nothing's changed." After a few sessions, Petra told me she submitted her resignation and much to her surprise her boss and her boss's boss met with her to discuss her decision. "I guess I got their attention. When I repeated what my issues were, they agreed to work with me on a plan of action to address my concerns. The meeting was incredibly productive."

Many single people are often afraid to "rock the boat" because they are solely financially responsible for rent or mortgage payments, car payments, insurance, entertainment and travel expenses, etc. Generally, they don't have another income to count on as back up so it's often easier to take the path of least resistance and stay in a job that's a major obstacle to a balanced life -- again, another tough choice. A helpful strategy in making a decision about your job involves four steps: acknowledge the problem, communicate the problem as well as possible solutions to management, wait to see if change occurs, and then make the appropriate decision to stay or to leave.

Many organizational cultures expect single people to be more flexible with their work and week-end schedules assuming that they have fewer responsibilities and stresses outside of work. I say nay! Single individuals have different responsibilities and stresses. Dealing with parental expectations, riding the emotional roller coaster of dating, maintaining friendships, being a good friend, focusing on professional and personal development, etc. etc., all of which keep their hamster wheels spinning faster and faster.

I have to admit that I, too, became oblivious to this group until one day a participant approached me and said, "I would get a lot more out of this if you could also address the challenges single people face in maintaining a balanced life." I was embarrassed at my lack of sensitivity. I asked her if she would be willing, after the break, to speak to the larger group about these issues based on her own experience. Fortunately, she agreed. The issues of work/travel expectations, social isolation, an overall lack of interest from her co-workers in her personal life, exclusion at work social events were a few that she touched on. She really spoke from her heart. When she finished the audience gave her a hearty round of applause. Those of us with families quickly forget what we went through when we were single.

As with Malti, I encourage singles to speak up and out at work. People need to be reminded and re-educated about the life balance issues singles face. It's your responsibility to keep our feet to the fire.

Support System

Cultivating a support system takes time and energy. "Ah, another thing to do," you say to yourself. Yes! This is a must do.

There are three key components to this quadrant. The first is support as reflected in household/childcare needs, the second is interpersonal relationships and the third deals with finances.

As for the first component, it's helpful to assess what, if any, household help/childcare needs you have. Since our lives can change so rapidly, periodically re-evaluating these needs is a must. It is sometimes so easy to get trapped into our routines that making a change can be tough.

Ellie, a thirty-year-old mother of two children ages one and three, approached me after one of my seminars. "I am constantly exhausted and irritable. I feel like I'm always yelling at the kids and my husband and he seems to be doing the same." Ellie and her husband purchased a new house nearer to their jobs, yet she wanted her two children to continue to attend a day care center near their old house, which is 45 miles from her job. She had to get up at 4:30 AM in order to get herself and the kids ready, drive them to day care and make it into work by 7:30 AM. Her husband picked the kids up at the end of the day.

I asked her if there wasn't another day care center nearer to her new house. "Well, yes there is and it's a very good one but the kids seemed to prefer the old one." I asked her if keeping them there was worth her exhaustion and crankiness. "Well, maybe not." Ellie and I talked about how she needed to re-evaluate the viability of this particular day care center and the toll it was taking on her and her family.

Singles also need to consider household support. A single thirty-eight-year-old VP of a Fortune 500 company told a group of her managers that she finally decided to hire a housekeeper. "Silly as it sounds I felt guilty for even thinking about it. But then I realized that I didn't want to spend my time cleaning so I broke down and hired someone. It was the best thing I've ever done!"

The main challenge for women in the Support System quadrant is something I've mentioned earlier – reaching out and asking for help. Too many of us see this as a weakness, feeling that we "should" just be able to do everything. Remember Dyan? She had a meltdown because she was angry with herself for not being able to do it all!

We also think that our loved ones "should" know what we need and want. Sally thought that by asking for what she wanted, it wouldn't "count." I hear that so often from women and I quickly remind them that by clearly communicating their wants or needs, there are no pent-up resentments and angers. And that's what really counts!

Just like women, men have difficulty asking for support. Actually, it doesn't even register on their radar screens. For women, asking for help means that they are falling short in the relationship, not being "good enough" partners, moms, co-workers, etc. For men, asking for help means that they are dependent and weak. Ok, I understand this has to do with socialization and some brain sex but I always challenge men that if they are unable to ask for support can they give support? And I mean more than financial support. This is the key question in the Support Quadrant for men. If they are giving support to their loved ones, their relationships will be more balanced and less strained.

The second component has to with interpersonal relationships -- friends—yes, girlfriends for women and male friends for men. Cultivating friendships with members of the same sex is an essential ingredient to experiencing balance. Men tend to seek out buddies that will often tell them what they want to hear. Further, men tend to keep their conversations focused on football scores or RBI's. They are more likely to talk to a woman about deeper issues or feelings since they wouldn't be risking compromising their masculinity. Again, I attribute this to socialization and brain sex. However, in my experience, of late, younger men are much more willing to be vulnerable seeking to get honest feedback and input. Having a confidante who will be honest with you is necessary for periodic reality checks.

We women are more likely to acknowledge or empathize with our friends and will seek diplomatic ways to confront when needed. In my view, female support and female friendships are critical to life balance. These relationships enrich our lives and these networks provide ways to learn about myriad things from finance to menopause.

When was the last time you had a night out with the girls?

As a result of one of my consulting jobs at a Fortune 500 company, I met three of the most wonderful women who had reached VP levels. We worked together to plan and execute a major work/life balance event. Afterward I suggested that we all go out to dinner one evening. Everyone agreed. We went to a local restaurant, drank some great wine and had so many laughs our sides were hurting. The next day I received a separate e-mail from each of them that basically said the same thing, "Thanks for suggesting dinner. I forgot what it was like to have girlfriends. When can we do it again?"

The last component to this quadrant has to do with finances. Many, many women I have worked with over the years have diminished their need to earn a competitive salary. They tend to be less assertive when salary negotiations and/or raises are discussed. They think that money is not what matters most. I've often heard, "Well, I really don't care what I earn as long as I like what I'm doing." This kind of mentality will keep this quadrant off balance. Being able to seek and pay for household support or childcare means women must care what they earn and aggressively seek fair compensation.

Early in my career when asked what my training or speaking fees were I generally felt my stomach constrict and I would quote a fee that was several hundred dollars less than the industry standard. And as the numbers rolled out of my mouth, they did so on a rising inflection as though I were questioning if I was really worth it! I somehow thought that I was being greedy if I commanded what others (mostly men) in my field were asking. I commiserated with my female colleagues who also struggled with this. One day as a group of us were complaining about fees over a bottle of wine, we decided we had to change our mindsets. We supported each other, role-played fee negotiations and stopped thinking that "money wasn't that important" or that we were being greedy. I never flinch over my industry standard fee anymore. I realized that money does matter and if this is being greedy, I like it!

So, examining your current and potential future compensation is a way to determine if your job supports your personal, childcare and household requirements.

Personal Care Resources

This quadrant is the cornerstone to experiencing a balanced life. Valuing yourself and putting yourself first benefits your family and loved ones. This was fully explored in Chapter Four. Another critical area I'd like to explore in this quadrant deals with stress.

Our bodies are one of our greatest resources when it comes to living a balanced life. However, most of us are spinning so fast on the hamster wheel, we aren't aware of our body's messages, at least not until we have a significant physical or emotional break down. Everyone's body reacts differently to prolonged periods of stress.

Do you know what your out-of-balance symptoms are? Whenever we're overdoing it, our bodies let us know. Go to Appendix I on pages 102 and 103 and complete the checklist. Periodically use this to keep yourself aware of your level of balance.

If you are present in your life, you will be much more alert to your out-of-balance symptoms and be able to respond effectively to them. If you have frequent headaches, or sleepless nights or if you experience a racing heart, stop and evaluate what's going on in your life. What is happening at home, at work or in your relationships? Are there any major changes occurring? When was the last time you nurtured yourself? What do you need from the people around you? What can you do differently?

Indra, a thirty-two-year-old married mother of three-year-old triplets sought counseling because she was having frequent migraines and becoming increasingly depressed. "I don't know what's wrong with me. I've never been sick. I'm usually a very energetic and resilient person. But lately, this depression and these headaches are really bringing me down." She sighed and said, "I don't know why this is happening."

As we talked, I learned more about her and how her life had changed over the past 12 months. Indra lost her position in a downsizing and had not been able to find a comparable one since. Her husband, who was a stay-at-home dad, had to get a job. She wept as she said, "The kids were shuttled off to day care, which really bothers us because we agreed that they would be raised by one of us. Then a few months ago, my mom was diagnosed with third stage breast cancer and I am taking care of her along with my dad who's an emotional basket case over her cancer." And she really believed there was no reason why she should be so depressed! She had not created space, pausing to reflect on what was happening and what she needed to do to take care of herself while she was taking care of everybody else! By not paying attention to her body soon enough, her symptoms became worse.

As we talked it became clear to both of us that one of her self-nurturing activities that fell by the wayside during all of this turmoil was her daily three-mile run. So that's the first thing she agreed to start doing again – no excuses. When she returned for her next visit, none of her situations had changed but she was feeling more in control and hopeful. Running was an important self-nurturing activity that replenished her body and spirit.

Let's take a BREATHE (5-6-8) break. Close your eyes and focus your awareness on your breath. Pay attention to the rising and falling of your chest and look for the spaces of peace in between your mental chatter.

Personal Qualities of Balanced Women

Many women I have worked with have asked the questions, "What is it about me that prevents me from having a more balanced life? The first step is to stop blaming themselves and start identifying what they can do to achieve their goals. Based on research and my observations of those women who have a greater sense of balance in their lives, there are nine personal qualities these women exhibit.

Having a sense of humor

In one study (McFarland & Wuest, 2003) women, ages 20-55, were asked what qualities best describe today's healthy woman. Humor was rated as *the* most important trait. Humor helps maintain perspective and lends itself to a light-heartedness in facing any life challenge. Keep in mind that laughter is good for the body. Laughter

- Decreases levels of stress hormones
- Increases pain tolerance
- Stimulates the muscular and skeletal systems
- Decreases heart rate
- Increases muscular and respiratory activity
- Stimulates the cardiovascular system, the sympathetic nervous system and the production of catecholamines
- Increases antibodies – the body's first line of defense against respiratory illness

And, did you know
- 100 laughs is equal to ten minutes of aerobic exercise?

Of the people who have sought counseling in my practice, the ones who concern me the most are those that are unable to laugh at themselves or at their situation. A mother who tragically lost her sixteen-year-old daughter in an auto accident was able to smile and laugh as she shared memories of their lives together. Through the course of counseling, she was able to channel her grief by spearheading a driver's education program for teens in her local community. Another client whose twenty-two-year-old son died from a work-related accident remained fixated in her anger and continued to be bitter and depressed. When I probed for positive memories, her anger always took precedence.

Laughter is about letting go – it's about being present. When we're laughing, we're in the moment, free from fear, anxiety or resentment. We're able to physically and emotionally connect with the positive aspects of our lives.

Women who are "doing addicted" don't' find much to laugh about. They take themselves and life way too seriously. One of my clients told her family that each had to tell a joke at the dinner table. At first, they balked but she said that within a few minutes, the whole family was laughing wildly at some of the silliest jokes. "It seemed to re-vitalize the entire family."

A family member of mine moved to Mexico. To keep his spirits up during the transition, I e-mailed him a "Joke of the Day" about three times a week. This forced me to find some good jokes! How can you incorporate humor into your daily life?

Having a spiritual side

One's spirituality is unique to the individual and is a deeply personal quest. Spirituality is essential to being balanced in that it provides a basis for a sense of purpose and meaning in life. Other benefits relate to one's overall health. Recent medical studies indicate that spiritual people exhibit fewer self-destructive behaviors, (i.e., suicide, smoking, and drug and alcohol abuse) less stress and a greater total life satisfaction. They also have also been shown to be less depressed, have healthier blood pressure levels and immune systems.

Maintaining a healthy, optimistic attitude

If you are optimistic, your life view is one that looks upon the world as a positive place. Optimists tend to believe that things will work out in the end. Keep in mind, however, that in psychological terms, optimism and pessimism do not function as opposites. Having more of one doesn't mean that you have less of the other. On many occasions in life, we need both. A 19th century writer and politician called for "pessimism of the intellect, optimism of the will." The one moves us to action while the other gives us the ability to believe that our actions will result in meaningful change.

Making time for yourself

Recognizing that your battery needs to be charged and recharged on a daily basis in order for you to be *truly* effective at home and at work is a great motivator for making time for yourself—no excuses! In order to feel that life is worth living, it's imperative that you replenish your physical and emotional energy reserves. Do you know what recharges you? What thought patterns emerge when you think about taking time for yourself? *"When* am I going to do that??" "I would need a month off to recoup." "That will never happen with my schedule." These unrealistic and negative thoughts only keep you stuck, exacerbating your fatigue and resentments. Look for solutions not excuses.

Being physically and nutritionally fit

We all know that we need to make healthy food choices and exercise regularly but we allow our "busy-ness" to be an obstacle. Food is frequently used as a reward for feeling overworked and underappreciated – it's an easy but unhealthy way to self-nuture. What eating and exercise goals have you set for yourself lately? Are they the same ones you keep promising yourself you'll do over and over again but never do? If so, get honest with yourself and take a personal inventory to assess, re-evaluate and perhaps modify these goals *GIVEN* your current life demands and responsibilities. Why keep breaking promises to yourself? This negatively affects your self-esteem and sets up a cycle of yo-yo dieting that only increases the likelihood of weight gain.

Years ago I decided that I would exercise every day by going to the local gym. I bought the clothes and the shoes and the gym bag. I looked like a real athlete and thought that this high priced work-out paraphernalia would surely motivate me. Each morning when the alarm went off, I groaned, turned it off and returned to my somnambulistic state. With each passing day I felt greater guilt so much so that I hid my work-out clothes. Then it dawned on me – I HATE gyms. When I realized that this choice was not realistic for me, I pondered what other options I had and I ended up buying a treadmill and a stationery bike. With the exception of vacations, I've rarely missed a day.

Creating Space for reflection

Making time for yourself is different than creating space for reflection. The former has to do with activities that relax and re-energize you. The latter has to do with solitude and quiet time. This is the most critical aspect of life balance. We move at high velocity to manage all of our roles and responsibilities and most often feel as though life is passing us by. Many of us drop into bed at night, dead with exhaustion, and can't even remember where the day went or what day it is.

Being present in your own life requires a discipline of awareness. It means stepping off the hamster wheel of daily responsibilities and interactions and realizing the miracle of your own life. A simple but powerful way to do this is to **breathe** slowly and rhythmically, continually focusing your awareness on your breath while at the same time tuning into your senses – what you're smelling, seeing, tasting, hearing or touching. Being still and quiet is very uncomfortable for most people. We are used to iPods, DVD's TIVO's, etc., etc. Our auditory space is filled with noise until we close our eyes to sleep.

Another strategy is to awake 15 minutes early and meditate, read an inspirational book or just be still while having a cup of coffee or sitting out in nature. During your drive time or on your walk or run, turn the radio off or ditch the iPod and do some reflective breathing in silence.

Knowing out-of-balance symptoms

Are you so busy and overwhelmed that you're not even aware that your body is giving you cues to slow down and take healthier courses of action? Some people have no awareness of their bodies – they live from the neck up. This is very dangerous and can lead to serious physical and emotional health problems. I've referenced the <u>Out-of-Balance Checklist</u> found in Appendix I on pages 102 and 103 earlier in this chapter. If you haven't taken it do so now and see how tuned-in you are to your body. Once you are aware of your symptoms, pay attention to your body's hot spots periodically throughout the day and see what needs attention. Then, take the appropriate action to ameliorate the symptom.

Setting boundaries

Boundaries are the guidelines we establish for ourselves and with others in order to maintain a healthy, balanced life -- personally, socially, and professionally. Boundaries are easily blurred when we can't say "no," or when we become overly involved in someone else's emotional space. Boundaries can be established directly or indirectly. Directly establishing boundaries involves both knowing and clearly communicating your needs, likes, dislikes, values, interests and availability to others and then clearly communicating them. Being ambivalent and nonassertive are indirect methods of setting boundaries.

Milan, a 51-year-old married mom of three, had to place her mom in a retirement community when her dad died. She was tearful as she talked about how overwhelmed she was with the demands her elderly mother placed on her. After some discussion in her table group at one of my seminars, she realized that she hadn't set any direct boundaries with her mom. Whenever her mom criticized her for not calling or visiting her more often, she promised to do better. Rather than being assertive and telling her mom exactly what she was able to do, Milan set indirect boundaries by making excuses and being ambivalent with her mom about her visits.

The group supported her in her decision to see her mom twice a week and limit phone calls to every other day unless it was an emergency. Some weeks after the seminar, Milan e-mailed me to tell me that she had a rough start with her mom who resisted the change. "But eventually my mom got the picture and actually began making friends at the retirement community. Even though I still feel some guilt, I recognize that I don't have to let it control me. As each day goes by, I'm feeling more and more in control of my life.

Effectively managing emotional health

Women experience depression and mood swings at twice the rate men do. This is primarily due to

> ➢ Biological factors, i.e., reproductive, hormonal, genetic,
> ➢ Cognitive styles (<u>Ruminative Thinking</u>), and a
> ➢ Higher incidence of psychological and economic stresses.

In addition, due to their relational nature, women will often repress or minimize their anger in order to preserve a relationship. Consequently, women have a different challenge than men do in being able to effectively manage their emotional health. The nine personal qualities listed above are tools that can assist them in this process.

Go to Appendix II on pages 106 – 108 to do a self-rating on the nine personal qualities. Which are your strengths? Which do you need to work on?

What's Your Passion?

"I have no idea what I'm passionate about." "I'm passionless." "I have no passion about anything except maybe my family." In my seminars, many women will tell me that they want to feel passionate about....something! Yet, they are unclear as to where their passions lie. What do you really, really care about? Passion is what brings great energy to your life. Think about what makes you light up and get excited. I will frequently ask women to think about when they were 10 or 11 and try to remember what they loved to do at that age. As girls enter adolescence they often give up these pre-adolescent activities in favor of make-up, clothes, friends, parties, boys, etc.

Recently widowed, Jo, a fifty-year-old woman with three grown children, sought counseling because her grief was overwhelming. Although we met for several months, I began to feel that I wasn't really helping Jo move along. She continued to isolate herself and dwell on her loneliness. I decided to switch gears and focus on something else, so one day I asked her what she liked to do when she was a pre-teen.

She looked off in reverie and then said, "Well, I used to play the piano. Actually, I kind of liked it. I don't know why I stopped."

"Well, why don't you take some lessons just to see how it feels again?" I asked.

At our next session, Jo was smiling and said, "Well, I went off the deep end. I not only took piano lessons, but I bought a piano and I've been playing every spare moment I have!" she exclaimed. "I feel alive. I never realized how passionate I was about music."

Our sessions became less frequent as Jo moved into the acceptance stage of grief. Her passion for music helped.

Another client of mine sang in the church choir as a pre-teen. So, she took voice lessons and connected with her passion for singing. Often, we have interests that we don't think of as passions, like gardening, knitting, etc. Take some time to reflect and you are likely to connect with what you are passionate about.

Recap

In conceptualizing balance, I have adapted some research conducted at Stanford University as well as my own research and co-developed a Four-Quadrant model that includes Family Resources, Support Resources, Work Resources, and Personal Care Resources. The mini-assessment survey, which you can use again and again as a reality check, will give you an idea of how you're staging overall work/life balance.

*If you would like to obtain a copy of the full length assessment, contact Dr. McFarland at bmcf@earthlink.net or visit her website at www.flexlifesolutions.com.

Seven

Awakening

Taking joy in life is a woman's best cosmetic.
Rosalind Russell

In order to determine a life balance baseline and assess progress, my colleague, Maria Arcocha White and I co-developed the FlexLife Assessment, a forty-item self-scoring questionnaire that determines the stage of balance you are in for each of the four quadrants. In concert with the assessment, people also have an opportunity to crystallize their core values within each quadrant.

This is the heart of the FlexLife: Choices and Strategies seminar I conduct. The assessment, which is a self-scoring instrument that provides participants with their level of balance in each of the four quadrants and a forced-choice checklist of core values that helps them evaluate how their core values align with their FlexLife Assessment results.

For our purposes, I'm going to ask you to first take the Forced Choice Core Values Checklist located in Appendix III on pages 110 – 111 which will give you an idea of your core values and which quadrants they tend to cluster in. Do you like what you see? If not, what do you need to do to have greater alignment with your life balance vision?

Now take the mini-assessment located in Appendix IV on pages 114 and 115 which will give you an overall work/life balance score. Once you've taken the mini-assessment, you should have an overall balance score that falls into Stage I, Stage II, Stage III or Stage IV which I describe below. I use this mini-assessment in my keynotes, and although the scores aren't as reliable as the longer assessment, it can give you a starting point as I discuss the stages below. If you wish, you can guess which stage you think you are in.

Keep in mind that these stages are pointers to keep you more present and awake in your life. They are not linear nor are they static or fixed. As with life itself, they can fluctuate from moment to moment, day-by-day, and are determined by your choices and decisions.

Stage I
The Hamster Wheel Stage
"No one can do it as well as I can."

You are living your life in a mindless trance! Perfectionism and "being all things to all people" can generate feelings of anger, resentment, disappointment and exhaustion. Asking for help or support is something you see as a weakness while doing anything for yourself is viewed as "selfish." You have a vision of balance floating around in your head but have never done a reality check on it. Thus, it's likely that there is a great disparity between what you think a balanced life *should be* and what your real life actually is. This disparity generates feelings of inadequacy and failure.

Taking great pride in multi-tasking and being able to do it all might precipitate periodic meltdowns and crying jags. These feelings, coupled with being unappreciated, may give rise to anger and resentment toward others. Saying "No" to anyone is most difficult for you because you are a people-pleaser. This tendency leads you to over schedule, overbook and be taken advantage of. Life becomes joyless yet, you keep trying harder and harder on the Doing Dimension, somehow hoping that your life will improve.

Beth Ann and Dyan were in this stage prior to counseling. You may want to reread their stories.

Emotions that characterize Stage I include resentment, anger, insecurity, defensiveness, depression, joylessness, exhaustion, unhappiness, as well as feeling under appreciated and overwhelmed. Women in this stage are so unaware, they are oblivious to their physical/emotional out-of-balance symptoms.

Stage Two
Crisis Stage
"Is this all there is?"

I call this the crisis stage. Hitting bottom *can* be positive. Perhaps you're having serious relationship issues, or experiencing physical problems such as frequent migraines or maybe you're depressed and feeling completely burned-out. Since this stage can be a catalyst for change, you might decide to seek counseling, talk to a spiritual advisor or to close friends. This is the space that can lead to self-reflection and self-evaluation as regards the quality of your relationships at home and at work and, most importantly, in your relationship with yourself. Although hitting bottom can be a turning-point, be careful. Many people become frightened as they face their feelings and the reality of their current life situations. They can slide back to Stage I. Stepping off the hamster wheel can be scary.

All of the cases I described in this book moved into Stage II when they sought counseling.

Emotions that may surface during Stage II include depression, burn-out, loneliness, self-doubt, as well as feeling trapped and out-of-control. Out-of-balance physical/emotional symptoms escalate in this stage. People in this stage are unable to ignore the symptoms any longer.

Stage Three
Awakening Stage
"I have what it takes to experience a balanced life."

Surges of empowerment are a direct result of your commitment to take care of yourself by identifying self-nurturing activities, by being more assertive and by taking responsibility for your choices and decisions. You are re-evaluating your values in every aspect of your life and re-negotiating necessary changes, resulting in greater clarity regarding your needs and wants. Now you not only know how to self-nurture but you also make the time to do it.

Be prepared, however! Your friends, family and co-workers may resist the new you! Your altered mindset will place greater responsibility on them to participate more and to do more for themselves. Although guilt feelings may increase in this stage, don't worry. They will pass as long as you stay the course you've set for yourself.

You're beginning to feel comfortable off the hamster wheel.

This stage was the aftermath for Liz. You may recall her new found empowerment led to other proactive decisions and a greater quality of life.

Feelings that characterize Stage III include relief, empowerment, joy, greater energy and sense of control and greater presence. Women in this stage respond quickly to their out-of-balance physical/emotional symptoms.

Stage Four
The Vibrant Stage
"I am there"

In this stage you are connected to your personal value system as you face the challenges life presents you. You make the time to reflect and self-evaluate on a regular basis, trusting others to be a part of this process. Recognizing that you are your most important person, you take responsibility for meeting your personal needs, set clear boundaries with others, and take immediate steps when you're sliding backwards. Solitude is something you're comfortable with and enjoy. Being in the moment happens more often than not. You feel great joy in the experience of your own special life and are able to laugh at yourself.

Feelings that characterize this stage include a zest for life, joy, greater presence, peace and contentment and a deeper spiritual connection. Women in Stage IV are fully connected to their bodies, making choices and decisions that promote physical/emotional health and well-being by eating right, exercising and managing their stressors.

Keep in mind that Stage IV isn't the "arrival" point. Being in a state of balance is fluid and ever changing. High achievers and perfectionists are prone to use this stage as a standard to measure themselves against which is very dangerous and unquestionably interferes with experiencing a balanced life.

I remind my seminar participants that these results can turn on a dime therefore, there is no resting on your laurels if you're at a Stage III or IV. Being conscious of the balance or lack thereof in each of the quadrants is what can lead you to make the tough choices necessary to return to equilibrium.

Let's take a BREATHE (5-6-8) Close your eyes and focus your awareness on your breath. Pay attention to the rising and falling of your chest and look for the spaces of peace in between your mental chatter.

Progress not Perfection

Unlike balance, which I believe can't be achieved but rather experienced, Stages III or IV can be achieved through conscious planning and responsible decision making. First we have to identify what, in each quadrant, is a resource or a liability.

FOUR QUADRANT WORK/LIFE BALANCE MODEL

Work Resources	Family Resources

Educational opportunities
Manageable travel
Available benefits
Career advancement opportunities
Challenging/meaningful work
Regular work hours
Autonomy
Flexibility
Mentor/Coach
Sense of being valued
	Physically and emotionally healthy
	  family members (nuclear and
	  extended)
	Positive, supportive & available
	  partner
	Supportive extended family
	Financial security

Support Resources	**Personal Care Resources**

Network of supportive and available
  female friends
Good and sufficient childcare/
  household help
Adequate financial resources
Ability to ask for help/support
Confidante or two
	Making time for yourself
	Being physically & nutritionally fit
	Setting clear boundaries with others
	Knowing out-of-balance symptoms
	Creating space for reflection
	Having a spiritual side
	Having a sense of humor
	Maintaining an optimistic attitude
	Effectively managing emotions

Go through the quadrants and feel free to add any other descriptors that may apply to your life. Place a plus (+) or a minus (–) by each descriptor. Then choose one minus (–) item from each quadrant.

In Appendix V on pages 118 – 121 you will find Action Plans to guide you in writing down the one area from each quadrant you would like to work on. Remember, if you don't record your goals, you will never realize them. It further helps if you verbally share your goal with someone.

Recap

In this chapter we looked at the Four Stages of Awakening.

Stage One	The Hamster Wheel Stage
Stage Two	Crisis Stage
Stage Three	Awakening Stage
Stage Four	Vibrant Stage

Eight

❁

The Balancing Act for Men

*A woman knows all about her children. She knows about
dentist appointments and romances, best friends, favorite
foods, secret fears and hopes and dreams. A man is vaguely
aware of some short people living in the house.*

Anonymous

As I mentioned in the Forward of this book, this revised and
expanded Second Edition has tried to be more inclusive of men
and the struggles they face as they search for life balance. I have
always been a believer in walking in someone else's shoes before
trying to fully understand another's feelings, decisions, actions, and
lifestyle. Through the challenges life has given me, I have been able
to walk in the shoes of many of my clients and with others whose
life experiences were unknowable by me, I connected through the
simple experience of being the same gender.

And although I have counseled and worked with men, I have
had to make a leap of understanding using my dad, my brother,
my husband, and my son as barometers for at least being able to
walk beside them as they shared their anger, frustrations, losses and
decisions. That said, although I can appreciate the struggles men
have with life balance, only another man can effectively express just
what those challenges are. So, I carefully thought about who I would

invite to share their life stories and perspectives on life balance. Although several people came to mind, I knew I had to include men who not only "talked the talk" but "walked the walk." Wanting to capture perspectives at different life stages, I invited a Gen Xer and a Baby Boomer to contribute.

They both are very busy individuals and when I asked if they had the time to share their viewpoints on life balance and at the same time meet a very tight deadline, they both said "Yes" without hesitation. Knowing how everyone struggles with balance, they were eager to share what has been most effective for them. I am pleased to introduce David Homan, a thirty-seven-year-old married dad with three tots – Sam, 6, Maura, 4 and Max, 2. He is the Director of Marketing and Client Services at McGohan Brabender, an employee benefits brokerage and consulting firm located in Dayton, Ohio. In this role David oversees all marketing, advertising and communication efforts for the company's three offices.

My second guest author is Mike Friedman a fifty-two-year-old married dad of two – Mariel, 20 and Zach, 16. Mike, a Director of Innovation Systems at Procter & Gamble, is responsible for improving how P&G innovates as a company around the world.

As I read and edited their contributions, I gained greater insights into the challenges that today's working dads face in achieving life balance. I have found throughout my travels that many baby boomers in my audiences make the assumption that women have greater struggles with life balance then do men. I must say that, I, too, have been guilty of such a mindset. Perhaps it's because we boomers grew up in families where the division of labor was more clearly defined and we conjecture that men are still primarily invested in their careers. Dave and Mike make the case that, although their jobs are important, they want a quality of life that allows them to be physically and emotionally healthy and to be integral and vital members of their families. Although they are unique individuals, their desire to lead balanced lives is not – regardless of gender or ethnicity, I believe we all want to experience vibrant, balanced lives where we are able to nourish and enjoy our family relationships and contribute at peak levels for our organizations.

A Man's Take on Life Balance
By
Dave Homan

My name is David and I am a recovering imbalanced husband, father and co-worker. It has been 8 months since my last confession… er, meltdown. The following story is true – the names have not been changed; however, for visualization purposes, please feel free to picture me as a cross between Brad Pitt and Johnny Depp.

Recently, my family was driving to Pittsburgh for a quick weekend getaway. With my kids watching a movie in the backseat and my wife taking a well-deserved nap, my mind wandered to thoughts of what was going on back at the office. What were my people working on? How many messages were in my voicemail? Did someone remember to post our press release on the website? Why hadn't anyone called me during the past couple of hours? Uh oh. I suddenly had an uneasy feeling in my stomach as I glanced down at my old friend, *Mr. Crackberry*. He smiled back – "Hello, friend. It's been far too long." I snapped my head back to the road but his voice continued: "What if you miss something urgent? What if they forgot about the press release? What if they all left for the afternoon and the department is empty? Come on friend – just one call -- one call won't hurt anything." As I could feel my anxiety reaching stroke level, I took a deep breath, (deciding not to close my eyes for obvious reasons), reached over and turned off Mr. Crackberry, and instead turned on the radio. *What a difference 10 months can make in a life.*

Hitting Bottom

Sometimes you just have to hit rock-bottom before you're ready (or able) to make a change in your life. For me, it happened the night of my office Christmas Party. After completing a stressful and exhausting week of work while battling a virus, the last place in the world I wanted to be was at a party that evening. However, my wife, Amy and I had made arrangements for the kids to spend a night at the grandparents, and since we hadn't had a night out without the kids since Watergate, I sucked it up.

Physically, I was present at the party. However, mentally I was a million miles away. After making the obligatory social rounds and feeling worse, I asked Amy if she was ready to go, and she said that was fine. Not even asking Amy what she wanted to do, I drove straight home to dead silence. I just assumed Amy was also tired from a pre-holiday week with the kids. At home though, I could see something was terribly wrong. So following the *"is something wrong"* interrogation for the fourth time, Amy justifiably unloaded on me.

The sum and substance of the conversation dealt with how we had wasted a night without the kids. Why hadn't we gone Christmas shopping -- or to a movie -- or just out for coffee? I tried to explain that I was physically and emotionally exhausted, but it didn't matter. At that moment, I could have told her we had just won the lottery -- it still wouldn't have mattered. I had let her down and I had let myself down.

How could things have gotten to this point? I was working harder than ever before in my life. Between self-imposed 15 hour work days, home projects, playing with the kids, family functions and social obligations, I was running at a hundred miles an hour, yet not accomplishing much. And even though I was physically present, I was rarely completely engaged. The harder I pushed, the worse the situation grew.

I looked over and saw Amy's glassy eyes. I had let her down. At that moment I realized that my life had reached the point where I was not the good husband, father, co-worker, or person that I had wanted to be.

The Brutal Facts

One of my favorite authors, Jim Collins, talks about *confronting the brutal facts of the situation.* This is exactly what I did the morning after the Christmas party debacle. I took an introspective look at where my life had gotten off track. In assessing the situation, I noticed that my balance started to shift following my mom's death fifteen months earlier. We were extremely close. She was a simply amazing woman. I have never met a more self-less, caring person, and she often helped bring stability and calmness to me when it was needed most.

Her death created a huge void in my life. To fill the emptiness, I tried to keep busy in any way possible – 24 hours a day. Normally a very good sleeper, I was now spending most of my nights staring at the ceiling. Each day, I found myself getting up earlier and earlier …5:30…5:00…4:30…4:00. My body needed the rest – I just wasn't listening.

At work, the extra hours weren't helping my productivity. For the record, I love everything about my job – the people, the opportunities, the variety, the challenges – even the occasional crisis management. Every day brings new and exciting opportunities. However, two issues at work that typically get me into trouble from time to time have to do with my *disease to please* and my problems with delegation.

I can't say no to anyone. Need help with a proposal? Sure. Can't find something? Let me help you. Your cat needs to be wormed? I can help. There is something about helping someone else out that gives me a natural high. When I was at the top of my game, I was able to keep up with these demands. Unfortunately, as the physical and emotional exhaustion mounted, it became more and more of a stressful, exhaustive strain. Additionally, because I always solved people's problems, this created a self-imposed dependency on me.

Senior management kept telling me to slow down as they could see the stress and exhaustion mounting, but that only pushed me harder to show them I could handle the workload. There were many days when I skipped lunch, instead opting for the drive-thru for a quick meal on my way to the next meeting. Unfortunately, my idea of a balanced meal was eating a Big Mac while driving the car and talking on the cell phone.

After completing a draining work day, I would arrive at home still unable to disengage from work, repeatedly checking voicemail and email throughout the evening. Between giving the kids a bath and working on a home project, I would be drawn to my computer and voicemail like a crack addict. It was just an anxiety that I might miss something important and let someone down.

I tried so hard to be available to Amy and the kids each night, but I was already worrying about what the next day held. Physically, I was also running on fumes. There were times when I could have easily fallen asleep while wrestling with the kids. By the time the kids were put to bed at night, I had nothing left to give to me...no time to read a book...certainly no energy to exercise...*just enough time to check email one more time before bed...*

Taking Care of Me

Change began when I realized I needed to become a more selfish person. I was spending so much energy on other people that I completely forgot about the most important person in the equation – me. I stopped making time for myself to recharge my internal battery, exercise, eat right or even rest. Although I could slowly see the pounds adding to my weight and the bags around my eyes getting darker, I kept promising myself "tomorrow I will make a change." But tomorrow became next week, and next week became next month. During the course of my imbalanced decline, I gained 75 pounds. Some of it was from depression, some was from eating fast food on the run, and some of it was from a lack of physical activity.

I started with diet and exercise, joining a weight loss program online and setting aside 30 – 40 minutes each day for cardio work. Although it took me a couple of weeks to adjust to the new regiment, I totally committed myself to making the change. When the weight started to come off and friends and family provided positive feedback, this fueled my efforts. In fact, during the first three months, I missed only one day of exercise. During that time I lost over 60 pounds through re-establishing a healthy diet.

Exercise became contagious for me. Previously, I hated to exercise, and because so many other areas of life were imbalanced, I never saw the payout. However, once the weight started to drop,

I noticed a couple other benefits. My energy levels and alertness increased, and my asthmatic condition improved. It appears that after a long vacation, my endorphins were back on the job.

As I felt better, I would increase the amount of time spent daily on exercise. To find the extra time for exercise, I started to go jogging at 5:00 AM. This has turned out to be a great decision in several ways. It provides alone time for me to clear my head, set my priorities for the day, and spend some quiet time in reflection and prayer – bringing balance to other areas of my life. Second, it alleviates the anxiety of trying to fit in the exercise time later in the day. And third, if I am dragging my fat butt out of bed at 5:00 AM to go jogging when it's 20 degrees outside, I am going to think twice before swallowing a Krispy Kreme at work! To date, I have lost 92 pounds through doing nothing more than eating healthy and raising my heart rate. *Personal balance – check!*

Letting go and Delegating

Work has been more of a challenge. I really had to re-engineer my plan of attack. So much had changed in the last three and a half years. With the growth and success of our organization, my department had grown from a staff of one to six in a relatively short period of time, branching out into several new areas. As my role in the department changed from a "doer" to that of a coach and mentor, I had resisted the transition. I had trouble letting go of projects and duties, which prevented my employees from taking complete ownership of their jobs (although they had the talent and capabilities). At the end of the day, this doubled my work load and slowed their professional development. At my worst, I estimate that I only delegated about 20 percent of what I should have been doing.

McGohan Brabender is a great organization, regularly named as one of the Top 10 Companies to Work for in Dayton, Ohio. They are employee-oriented and provide myriad resources and benefits to help their people grow – at work and at home. To this point, I had been too proud to take advantage of this offer. But in light of my will to change, I experienced a brief moment of humility and asked for help. Boy, did they come through. I was provided with access to both a personal development coach and job specific leadership training.

Through the coaching experience, I have learned to effectively delegate duties guilt-free, and effectively support an employee while allowing her to maintain ownership of a project. I really try to approach every instance of employee contact as a coaching or mentoring opportunity.

As far as the dreaded *disease-to-please* sickness, I now prioritize every request into one of four categories: Urgent-Important, Not Urgent-Important, Urgent-Not Important, and Not Urgent-Not Important and delegate 100 percent of the tasks that can be delegated. Another tool that is use is to simply say *"No, I'm sorry I can't help you with that issue right now, but this is where you can find the answer."*

Telling people *no* instead of fixing the problem was the hardest thing to change. I not only had to re-program myself, I had to re-program others who had become dependent upon me to solve their every issue. I no longer allow other people's inability to plan become my crisis. Over time, the line to my office has shrunk, and for the most part, everyone understands that when someone is at my door, they need immediate attention.

The other major side effect that occurred in my department as a result of these changes? We got crazy again. Laughter, smiles, high-fives and practical jokes all make the day fly-by, and we often have employees from other departments visit us when they are having a bad day. I reconnected with how important laughter and smiles were to enjoying my work life and my co-workers as well as recharging my battery. This is something Barbara frequently emphasizes in her keynotes and talks about in Chapter Six.

It was amazing that with these slight changes, I was getting back at least one hour a day which helped me produce results for the organization and grow my people. *Work balance – check!*

The Family

I am going to be honest, once personal balance and work balance came into focus, home balance was a piece of cake. The rules I applied were simple. When I leave work, I mentally leave work. The more I check email and voicemail at home, the more I get drawn into issues and worries that can't be dealt with until the next day. So, I only allow myself to check messages or email if I know something is urgent. And I only check email once the kids are in bed. When I am at home, I am now mentally present or *there*. Something I heard Barbara speak about but was slow to put into practice! By focusing my attention on the present moment using an awareness of my breath, I have come to be more connected to myself and my family.

Also, I make sure that Amy and I have our time away from the kids, and more importantly, she has her time away from all of us. For example, every Saturday morning I take the kids out to breakfast alone and then we go somewhere or work on a project together which gives me uninterrupted, quality time with them. But more importantly, it gives Amy some much needed respite time alone. If I get home from work and Amy has "that look on her face," I tell her to go to Starbucks and leave the kids at home. I full well know that when Mommy's happy – everybody's happy! *Home balance – check!*

OK, so I guess I have it all figured out – wrong! You won't find me doling out advice on Oprah about work-life balance. I'm about as qualified to do this as Tom Cruise is to speak about post-partum depression; however, I do think there are some subtle differences regarding work-life balance as seen through the eyes of this man.

Men tend to be very task-oriented when it comes to life balance. Our successes are based almost entirely on achieving the desired end result. We are so driven to achieve a particular goal, we often pay little if any attention to the journey along the way. Because of this, we tend to live for the future, not the present. It can be stressful for us to live in the present because it distracts us from the goal at hand. Unfortunately, some of life's greatest moments and memories are created on the journey. When I would talk to my mom about something, I would always get straight to the point – the bottom line. Conversely, when she would tell me a story, it would include a story within a story within another story. I would get impatient and speed her along to the crux of the story. The end result was important to me, the journey was the important part of the story to her. My mom was living in the moment.

For men, balance is something that is measured and tangible, i.e., the mortgage is paid off, the project is done at work, etc. If I can't measure it, I can't manage it, therefore, it can't possibly help bring balance to my life. Conversely, women don't necessarily need to measure or see something for that balance to exist. Again, it goes back to living in the present, and the peace that accompanies it is where the balance is achieved.

Lean on Me

Building a strong support system is important for a balanced life. More importantly, though, you have to be able to reach out to them. The male ego is fragile and asking for help can be very emasculating – especially when it's confiding in another man. No man wants to be Clark Kent – he wants to be Superman. Let's face it, there will never be a commercial of two men walking on the beach with one man looking over and saying, "Earl, do you ever have that not-so-balanced feeling in your life?" On the other hand, I think women are more comfortable sharing their emotions and problems with others, and actually feel empowered by the situation.

While I am still a man in transition, today I am a better husband, father, co-worker and person. There are still days and situations where it is easy to fall back into old habits, but that is just the reality of the situation, and this is life – not *The Brady Bunch*! There are mornings where I don't want to get out of my warm bed and there are occasions at work where it is easier to simply do something rather than explain why and how to do it. These are the tough choices that are required in order for me to have a balanced life. When I make the choices that are aligned with my values, I feel the greatest triumph on my journey towards balance.

There is no greater feeling in the world than when I see my children and the neighborhood kids waiting for me in the driveway at the end of the day so I can play kickball with them – and now I do it without being worried about voicemail, deadlines or lack of energy!

HOW PETE SEEGER AND HARRY CHAPIN KEEP ME IN BALANCE

By
Mike Friedman

Let me introduce myself.

I am a mid-west surfer, miles from the ocean; an avid skier, far from the mountains; an engineer, who has never practiced engineering; a Latin culture lover, searching for people with whom to speak Spanish; a youth football, basketball and lacrosse coach, whose children no longer require parental sports coaching; a 29 year veteran of Procter & Gamble, who is now retiring; a lover of music, who has had a start/stop journey playing guitar and piano; a maturing student, always interested in learning something new; a passionate parent, striving to find the right balance between discipline and punishment; and a very lucky guy to be married for over 23 years to a wonderful woman and looking forward to the next 40!

How do I strive to maintain a balanced approach to work and life? It requires a lot of effort! I have been helped by using my upbringing and learning experiences to create a clear written vision of what is important to me in living my life: who I want to be, what I want to do and what goals I want to achieve. I have also been helped by regularly reviewing my actions in light of this written document to assess how I am doing and then talking over the good and the bad with a great partner, my wife, Helayne. Here is the story of my work life balance journey.

Early Influences

As I began defining my life vision, I was influenced by many of the experiences I had growing up in rural Pennsylvania and later at college in up-state New York. Some were good, some were bad, but, taken as a whole, they helped me think through what was important to me. Two things had particularly strong influences on me.

The first happened when I was in third grade. I got hopelessly behind in a Social Studies project outlining the history of Pennsylvania. I was failing the course. My teacher called my mom complaining about my academic shortcomings. I remember being a nervous wreck. My mom sat down with me and helped me catch up on the late assignments. I turned in the work and ended up with a "D" versus the more dreaded consequence of having to repeat third grade. This experience taught me two things: first, how critical it is to be proactive, even on tasks I didn't particularly enjoy or like and secondly, the importance of kind and caring, yet firm parental support. Of course, these insights came to me way after the trauma, but the memory sticks with me.

The second influence was music since it had always been a major part of my early youth and young adulthood. For most of us, certain songs capture our feelings at specific times in our lives and bring back very strong, emotional memories. This was definitely true for me. Two songs that I connected with are "Turn! Turn! Turn! (to Everything There Is a Season)," written by Pete Seeger and made famous by The Byrds in October 1965 and the other is "Cat's in the Cradle," by Harry Chapin.

'Turn! Turn! Turn!' brings back memories of the end of the decade of the 1960s. I was in high school dealing with what most high school kids of that era were – Vietnam, college, and what I wanted to do with my life. I struggled with so many issues -- I wanted to work to have money but I wanted a job that would help me get into a good college to become an engineer; I wanted to surf around the world, but couldn't because I had to train to get better at track; and I couldn't leave home because I had to help my Dad and brother care for my Mom who had been diagnosed with cancer. The emotional turmoil of these struggles were ameliorated by the freeing feeling I experienced when I heard the song. Those words helped me build into my life vision the notion that I didn't have to do everything at once. I realized that it was ok to make choices and that there would be more opportunities to do things in the future which I couldn't do today.

Cat's In the Cradle" brings back fond memories of my father and the things we did together: the first time he let me mow our yard on a riding tractor, watching to make sure I was safe; the times we went fishing early in the morning even though we rarely caught any fish; the purchase of my first condo in Huntington Beach, California. My dad co-signed for the mortgage even though he thought the interest rate was too high at 8%. For my dad, family came first and foremost – above any career advancement at Link-Belt where he was an engineer. So, when he had his long fight with cancer and our roles were reversed, I spent a lot of time with him. During those times, I realized I would be a father as he was to me -- always there no matter what. So, in defining my life vision I knew work would be important but the priorities of family were clear for me.

These influences crystallized my values and priorities but I didn't quite know how to put it all together in a clearly defined way.

Converting Life's Lessons into a Written Vision Statement

I had the good fortune to attend a number of personal development seminars at Procter & Gamble together with my wife, Helayne Angelus, which gave us the framework to flesh out our life visions. I believe that in order to experience a balanced life, it's essential to first develop a life vision. So, for me, my life vision consists of three major elements that include:

(1) A statement that addresses my need to be physically and mentally strong and alert.

(2) A series of affirmations discussed in Stephen Covey's *Seven Habits of Highly Successful People* which focus on being proactive, setting goals and priorities, having a positive attitude, being a good communicator, and taking care of myself physically, emotionally and intellectually.

(3) An outline of what I want to be, do and achieve in the most important roles in my life, which include father, spouse, son, and brother.

Since I find this last aspect of my life vision so helpful in balancing my life, I've included it below so the readers may have an example to use in developing their own.

Life Vision in My Key Roles

Father, Spouse, Son, Brother –
What I want to BE

- o A supporter, friend, coach and lover of Helayne

- o A teacher, emotional supporter, playmate and provider for my children.

- o A supporter, confidante, morale builder and counselor for my parent and in-laws.

What I want to DO

- o Spend quality time with Helayne, Zachary and Mariel.

- o Help Helayne deal with the challenges stresses and strains of being a mother and worker.

- o Help provide Mariel and Zach with the opportunities to grow, experience life and have fun.

Goals

Attend at least four school functions for Zach and Mariel.
Take five family vacations
Visit in-laws and parent three times a year
Take six special trips with Helayne

These are the details behind my first life role. I also have outlined similar descriptions for what I want to BE, what I want to DO, and what I want to accomplish over the next year for six other life roles which include Laborer, Manager, Designer at home; Manager at Procter & Gamble; Entrepreneur; Physical Health; Mental Health; Emotional Health.

How This Helps Me Achieve Balance

Eight years ago, I was playing the piano and guitar diligently, living a life-long dream. An opportunity arose to coach my son's lacrosse team which would prevent me from pursuing my musical passion. There was not enough time to do both. I chose to coach because it was very clear from my life role of dad that this is what I wanted to BE: teacher, emotional supporter, playmate and provider for my children. While I missed playing the music, in the shadows of my mind I often intermittently heard the words to the Harry Chapin and Pete Seeger songs. I felt at peace with my decision. I have the most wonderful memories of that time with my son.

Aside from coaching, in my role as a dad, my goal was to attend all of Zach's and Mariel's sporting events. This sometimes conflicted with travel plans for work, but I was not going to be "the father that didn't have time for his son." I delayed business travel to off-season times, did the work via phone or just turned down trips. Sometimes, I took the red-eye to get back in time. As President of my Temple, it was important for me to go to Friday night services. This conflicted with Zach's football games. My solution was to attend services from 6:15 PM to 7:00 PM and then leave early to go to Zach's game. Even though I was a little rushed, I felt comfortable with my choice and how it fit with my life vision.

While we all have different sets of experiences that influence our thoughts and feelings, achieving balance is a challenge. I find it requires constant reflection on what is important to me and the vision I have for what I want to do in my life. At the end of the day, it is about getting clear on the choice, the consequences of that choice and getting comfortable with the outcomes.

I mentioned earlier that my wife, Helayne, also attended the development seminars with me at Procter &Gamble. Being able to share our life visions and goals has been a big plus in achieving work life balance. Talking these visions out together has helped each of us clarify our priorities.

Helayne also works for Procter &Gamble and we have had many discussions on how to balance our careers. We decided when we got married that our relationship was most important to us and from that core value we created a vision for our future. Once we internalized what we each wanted, shared it with each other and then tested it against career opportunities, making choices became much easier and more comfortable. For example, I was offered an assignment to move to Caracas, Venezuela without Helayne understanding her career options. Our vision was win/win for both of us. We agreed that we would never live apart even if we had to give up a career opportunity that was good for one of us. So, we chose not to move until Helayne found a job that was right for her; and we were not going to commute, no matter how important the business need. It took time, but Procter & Gamble found a great role for Helayne. We moved to Caracas and it was a wonderful experience for all of us, including our children. Achieving balance was easier, because we had a framework for evaluating the decision and for discussing it, with a clear understanding of the pros and cons. We eliminated conflict in advance by thinking it through and then committing to our vision.

Raising children is filled with choices, the impact of which is difficult to see until much later. Again the Seven Habits training helped us think about how to make choices consistent with our principles and values which I discussed earlier. The values related to my children are repeated below.

What I want to BE

- o A teacher, emotional supporter, playmate and provider for my children.

What I want to DO

- o Help provide Mariel and Zach with the opportunities to grow, experience life and have fun.

Anchoring the choices to a set of principles that we had discussed in advance such as responsibility, personal accountability, persistence in achieving goals and growth through learning experiences helped reduce the guilt of "Are we doing the right thing?" We make a decision and move on. Then, when we wonder if it was the right decision, and begin to drift out of balance, we talk with each other, review principles and get back into balance.

An example we have wrestled with is how much allowance to give our daughter in her second year at college. We know that an extravagant allowance builds bad habits on her part and makes accountability difficult. More is not always the answer. When it is her own money and that's all she has, she makes much better and more thoughtful spending choices. So, Helayne and I talk through our viewpoints, get aligned and then talk with Mariel. She gives us her input. Our discussion is based on our principles. So we talk about Mariel's responsibility, personal accountability, persistence in achieving her goals and growth through learning experiences and then, together, we come to a mutually acceptable decision. And, when Mariel tries to push the envelope, Helayne and I have made a pact to talk it over together, reconnect with the guiding principles and then make our decision with one voice. That lessens the self-doubt and strengthens our commitment about our decision. Agreed upon principles, discussion with a partner, input from the kids, reflection and choice make parenting a lot easier.

Personal Balance

I mentioned earlier that my life vision consists of three major elements and that one of them included a statement that addresses my need to be physically and mentally strong and alert. This vision statement is the heart of personal balance for me.

The personal side of balance has always been easier for me. I really don't feel "guilt" around the expectations of others as to what I should or should not be doing. That allows me to be in the moment and not outside it, wondering what someone else would think of my choice.

Exercise is a very important part of being balanced as it has always helped me deal with conflicts. When I sense I'm getting out-of-kilter, I quickly realize that I have missed too many training sessions. Regular exercise makes me feel better physically and mentally and makes it easier for me to feel centered. I regularly mix weights with cardio with stretching and with Yoga. I do this as much as possible with Helayne so it is a shared activity. Sharing my personal balance needs with Helayne and my children helps because they then have a greater understanding of what drives some of the choices I make.

Gender Differences

It is interesting to reflect on male/female differences. I can only share my personal observations versus any statistical analysis. One perceived difference is that women are multi-taskers and men are more singularly focused. In some ways this may be true, as women seem to feel guilty because they are trying to do many things at the same moment, versus many things over one time period. One approach I use to help me do more than one task at the same time is finding ways to do things that meet multiple life roles. A simple thing like Helayne and me walking our dogs together on the weekends fulfills two of the goals of my Vision statement -- exercise and spending time with my wife. It brings me peace of mind to know that I am doing two of my most important life roles. I chose not to play golf because, while it would provide exercise, it would take me away from Helayne, since she doesn't play.

We are all familiar with the commonly joked about distaste men have for asking for directions. This rings true for me. I know for many years I fit that description. When Helayne used to kid me about that, it caused me to reflect on my behavior. "Why didn't I ask for directions?" So, now, whenever I get in a situation where I need to ask for help, I challenge myself –"Why aren't you asking?" This has changed my behavior. I no longer fit the paradigm of men less likely to seek support. At least, I am a lot better than I used to be!

My life is not all the things I want it to be all the time. It has the potential to get out of balance quickly. But I have found that a clear vision of what I want, what my priorities are, and a partner to help me think it all through, all anchored by good physical and mental health have enabled me to better achieve a good life work balance. And those Pete Seeger and Harry Chapin songs continue to be the threads that tie it all together.

* * * * * *

Although Dave and Mike's journeys are very different, their perspectives share a common theme – life balance is about making day-to-day choices that are based on core values. I know that both of these gentlemen work very hard on the Doing Dimension but know when to step off and BE.

Nine

❀

The Now of It All

*Today a new sun rises for me; everything lives, everything
is animated, everything seems to speak to me of my
passion, everything invites me to cherish it.*
Anne De Lenclos

Of the essential ingredients to experiencing a balanced life --
being *there*, valuing ourselves, reconciling our balance vision and
determining our life balance resources -- the most significant is
being *there,* being present and in the moment of our lives. What's
the point of having a balanced life if we're not present in that life?

Eckhart Tolle, author of *The Power of Now*, says that our lives
are perfect just as they are right now in the present moment. He
goes on to say that it is our life situations that are not. Many of
us keep trying to make our life situations "perfect" amidst much
frustration and angst. If we can, periodically throughout the day,
ignore the mental noise and pay deep attention to the miracle of our
own breath, we will experience balance and centeredness. If we
can pay deep attention to the people in our lives and to the world in
which we live, we will be living our lives to the fullest.

*   *   *   *   *   *

When I was a child, my parents encouraged me to take piano lessons to which I eagerly agreed. I wasn't very good but I so enjoyed banging on those ivory keys. My mother loved the song Beautiful Dreamer so I practiced and practiced until I thought I could play it flawlessly.

I ran into the kitchen where the smells of my mother's cooking stirred up hunger pangs. The stovetop was filled with large covered steaming pots, which she periodically checked in the middle of chopping some vegetables. "Mom," I blurted, "I have a surprise for you! Come and hear me play." She looked at me and then at the stove top and then at her vegetables and finally at the clock and said, "Right now?" "Yes, right now." I was afraid that somehow my fingers wouldn't be able to remember how to miss my usual mistakes. "Oh all right," she said with a deep sigh.

I took her hand and sat her down on the couch. While I was playing, I glanced over and noticed that although she was sitting there, she really wasn't *there*. She was still in the kitchen thinking about those pots and what time it was. I felt so deflated.

Let's fast forward to a few years ago when this memory burst out of the recesses of my memory bank. It was Thanksgiving and my entire family was celebrating it at my house. I was feverishly slaving in the kitchen, when my mother, who was 93 at the time, came up to me and said, "Barbara, how about playing the piano for me?" Somewhat irritated, I said, "Mother, I'm in the middle of dinner," and it was at that very moment I had my Beautiful Dreamer flashback.

I stopped what I was doing, took my mother by the hand and escorted her to my piano room. As I played, I glanced over and she was *there*—ever present, enjoying every moment. Are you going to wait until you're 93 to be *there,* to be fully present as you live your life?

Appendix I

Out-of-Balance Symptom Checklist

Check the out-of-balance symptoms you have noticed lately in yourself:

PHYSICAL

____ appetite change	____ colds	____ Rash
____ headaches	____ muscle aches	____ Foot tapping
____ tension	____ digestive upsets	____ teeth grinding
____ fatigue	____ pounding heart	____ weight change
____ insomnia	____ accident proneness	
____ finger drumming	____ increased drug, alcohol, cigarette use	

EMOTIONAL

____ anxiety	____ nightmares	____ nervous laughter
____ frustration	____ crying spells	____ worry
____ the "blues	____ irritability	____ discouragement
____ mood swings	____ "no-one cares"	____ little joy
____ bad temper	____ depression	

SPIRITUAL

____ emptiness	____ martyrdom	____ apathy
____ loss of meaning	____ desire for magic	____ cynicism
____ doubt	____ loss of direction	
____ lack of forgiveness	____ need to "prove" self	

MENTAL

____ forgetfulness	____ lethargy	____ negative self-talk
____ dull senses	____ whirling mind	____ spacing out
____ low productivity	____ no new ideas	____ confusion
____ negative attitude	____ boredom	
____ poor concentration	____ fewer contacts with friends	

RELATIONAL

____ isolation	____ Lashing out	____ nagging
____ intolerance	____ Hiding	____ distrust
____ resentment	____ clamming up	____ lack of intimacy
____ loneliness	____ lowered sex drive	____ using people

Appendix II

Nine Personal Qualities

Self-Rating Scale

1 = NOT AT ALL
10 = 100%

MAKES TIME FOR SELF   1...2...3...4...5...6...7...8...9...10

Do you know how to self-soothe or self-nurture? Even if you do, that's only half the challenge. You need to have a routine of replenishing your energy reserves and make this activity a priority in your life. No Excuses!!

**KNOWS OUT-OF-
BALANCE SYMPTOMS**   1...2...3...4...5...6...7...8...9...10

Are you tuned into your body? Are you listening when your body speaks to you about being stressed out? Headaches? Back Aches? Irritability? Do you have a stress reduction plan to help your body and mind get back into balance? Do you USE it???

**PHYSICALLY &
NUTRITIONALLY FIT**   1...2...3...4...5...6...7...8...9...10

If a woman is not fit or making healthy food choices, it's difficult to live a balanced life. Do you exercise regularly? Do you generally make healthy food choices? Do you have regular check-ups?

**HAVING A SENSE OF
HUMOR**   1...2...3...4...5...6...7...8...9...10

Being able to laugh at life and at oneself is critical to enjoying the ride! Taking life too seriously makes it less enjoyable and zesty! How zestful are you? How often do you laugh throughout the day?

EFFECTIVELY MANAGES
EMOTIONS 1...2...3...4...5...6...7...8...9...10

Women frequently have difficulty expressing their anger constructively. They tend to want to avoid conflict in order to preserve a relationship. In addition, women are prone to mood swings and depression. Do you know what you need to do to effectively manage these emotions when they become overwhelming? Would you seek professional help? Would you be willing to consider medication if recommended by your physician?

MAINTAINS A HEALTHY
OPTIMISTIC ATTITUDE 1...2...3...4...5...6...7...8...9...10

Do you tend to look at the bright side of things? Or are you a doom and gloomer?? Negative Nancy? Pay attention to your thoughts and neutralize the negative ones. Do you generally tend to see what's wrong with things rather than what's right?

SETTING BOUNDARIES 1...2...3...4...5...6...7...8...9...10

Do you know when someone is taking advantage of you or of your time? Are you able to say 'no' when it is in your own best interest? Boundaries are guidelines that people establish for themselves in order to be emotionally healthy and to maintain healthy, reciprocal relationships.

CREATES SPACE FOR
REFLECTION 1...2...3...4...5...6...7...8...9...10

Do you take time throughout the day to just "Be." A quiet walk, or a yoga practice or a meditation time are ways to be with yourself in solitude. Are you comfortable in silence?

HAS A SPIRITUAL SIDE 1...2...3...4...5...6...7...8...9...10

Having spiritual beliefs or a structured faith provides an inner strength. For many, spirituality is a work in progress. How often do you tap into your spirituality? Do you rely on it in times of difficulty? Do you have a set of spiritual practices that are meaningful for you?.

Appendix III

Forced-Choice Core Values Checklist

Circle 10 of your core values and then rank order them in importance to you.

Professional Success
Recognition
Status
Career Advancement
Challenging and meaningful work
Strong Work ethic
Professional Growth
Financial Success
Opportunity to contribute
Team player
Positively influencing others
Giving of self
Interdependence
Genuineness (direct communication)
Commitment
Financial Security
Being a positive & supportive partner
Having a positive & supportive partner
Kindness
Strong family relationships
Friendship
Empathy
Trust
Respect for others
Loyalty
A positive network of friends
Asking for help and/or support
Financial responsibility for future
Peace
Spirituality
Joy
Self-Care
Health
Self-Respect
Knowing/living my passion in life
Personal Growth
Humor
Optimism

Go on to the next page and see in which quadrants your core values fall.

The list of values have been categorized into the 4 Life Balance Quadrants. Find your 10 core values to determine which quadrant(s) they fall in.

Core Values

<ins>Work</ins>	<ins>Family</ins>
Professional Success	Positively influencing others
Recognition	Giving of self
Status	Interdependence
Career Advancement	Genuineness (direct communication)
Challenging and meaningful work	Commitment
Strong Work ethic	Financial Security
Professional Growth	Being a positive & supportive partner
Financial Success	Having a positive & supportive partner
Opportunity to contribute	Kindness
Team player	Strong family relationships
<ins>Support</ins>	<ins>Personal</ins>
Friendship	Peace
Empathy	Spirituality
Trust	Joy
Respect for others	Self-Care
Loyalty	Health
A positive network of friends	Self-Respect
Asking for help and/or support	Knowing/living my passion in life
Financial responsibility for future	Personal Growth
	Humor
	Optimism

How balanced are your core values?
Does your daily life reflect these values?
Are you making life balance decisions that are in alignment with these values?

Appendix IV

———— ❀ ————

*Flex*life Mini-Assessment

This mini-assessment will give you a baseline to determine which stage of work/life balance you're in at this point in time. Keep in mind, whatever your score on this instrument, it is just a mini-check on your *overall* level of balance. The longer version provides a score in each quadrant plus an overall score.

Your score can change from day to day, so unfortunately, if you're in Stage III or IV today, you may not be tomorrow. No resting on your laurels! If you're in Stage I or II, don't fret. That can change just as quickly. Re-taking either assessment can be used as a way to keep you focused and help you stay on track.

Your score will fall into one of four stages, which are described in Chapter Seven.

How Are You Staging On Work / Life Balance?
Work / Life Balance Mini Survey

Instructions:
Please circle the response that best fits the statement below.

0 Not at all or never true
1 Rarely true
2 Sometimes true
3 Often true
4 Almost always or always true

1	My job affords me the flexibility/autonomy I need to have a balanced personal family life.	0	1	2	3	4
2	I do not give up personal and/or family commitments for my work, and do not feel guilty during the times in which I must.	0	1	2	3	4
3	I have a good sense of humor.	0	1	2	3	4
4	I know what I need to do to take care of myself and feel good about making the time to do so.	0	1	2	3	4
5	I do not deprive myself to please others.	0	1	2	3	4
6	My partner (and/or family) contributes as much as I do to the responsibilities we have.	0	1	2	3	4
7	My partner/family is available and is a positive support to me as I pursue my personal/professional goals.	0	1	2	3	4
8	I have someone to call when I need to talk.	0	1	2	3	4
9	I have adequate household help/childcare/eldercare.	0	1	2	3	4
10	I feel confident and healthy in asking for help whenever I need it.	0	1	2	3	4

Add up your total score for all the questions.
TOTAL:

_____

OVERALL WORK / LIFE BALANCE SCORE		
Stage 1	=	0-16
Stage II	=	17-23
Stage III	=	24-28
Stage IV	=	29+

Appendix V

Action Plans

Action Plan
Quadrant One
Work Resources

1. I will work on

_____

_____

_____

2. The strategy I intend to use is...

_____

_____

_____

3. Take out your planner and schedule this strategy into your
   planner for the upcoming week.

_____

_____

_____

4. My greatest obstacle will be...

_____

_____

_____

5 I will deal with this obstacle by...

_____

_____

_____

6. My greatest support will be...

_____

_____

_____

Action Plan
Quadrant Two
Family Resources

1. I will work on

_____

_____

_____

2. The strategy I intend to use is...

_____

_____

_____

3. Take out your planner and schedule this strategy into your planner for the upcoming week.

_____

_____

_____

4. My greatest obstacle will be...

_____

_____

_____

5 I will deal with this obstacle by...

_____

_____

_____

6. My greatest support will be...

_____

_____

_____

Action Plan
Quadrant Three
Support Resources

1. I will work on

---

2. The strategy I intend to use is...

---

3. Take out your planner and schedule this strategy into your planner for the upcoming week.

---

4. My greatest obstacle will be...

---

5 I will deal with this obstacle by...

---

6. My greatest support will be...

Action Plan
Quadrant Four
Personal Care Resources

1. I will work on

_____

_____

_____

2. The strategy I intend to use is...

_____

_____

_____

3. Take out your planner and schedule this strategy into your
   planner for the upcoming week.

_____

_____

_____

4. My greatest obstacle will be...

_____

_____

_____

5 I will deal with this obstacle by...

_____

_____

_____

6. My greatest support will be...

_____

_____

_____

About the Author

Dr. Barbara McFarland, EdD, is a psychologist, author, trainer, media guest, and motivational speaker who has been enhancing the lives of women for nearly 25 years. Dr. McFarland has authored and co-authored 7 books some of which include *Feeding the Empty Heart* (Hazelden, 1984); *Shame and Body Image* (Health Communications, 1991); *Brief Therapy and Eating Disorders* (Jossey Bass, 1995, translated into Japanese); *My Mother Was Right! How Today's Women Reconcile with Their Mothers* (John Wiley; 1997, translated into Taiwanese); *Take Back Your Life NOW! Master the Ten Traits of Today's Healthy Woman* (First Books, 2003) is research-based and has been endorsed by former ABC Medical Correspondent, Dr. Nancy Snyderman, Senator Bob Dole, and iVillage Resident Physician Dr. Holly Atkinson.

She has also written many articles on various women's issues including one on body image which was published in *Oprah Magazine.* In addition, she counseled women in her private practice for nearly 25 years, pioneered the treatment of women and eating disorders, was invited to present her clinical work at Harvard University Medical School, Department of Psychiatry, conducted corporate training classes as part of the Xavier Consulting Group and presented keynote speeches at many women's health conferences. She also attended the Mental Research Institute at Stanford University to study brief therapy.

Dr. McFarland has conducted large-scale wellness programs and events at the Health Alliance, Procter & Gamble, General Electric, Ernst and Young, The Andrew Jergens Company, and Brown Foreman. She has worked extensively with Anthem Blue Cross & Blue Shield and Jones of NY on their Healthy Woman and Work/Life Balance programs. In 2005, she was the resident expert for Procter & Gamble's multi-brand website, www.perspectivesofbeauty.com.

Dr. McFarland has appeared on **Oprah, The Today Show, Diane Rehm** of NPR and PBS, as well as many others.

Barbara lives in Burlington, Kentucky, with her spouse, Harold and their awesome dog, Fred. Their awesome son, Casey, lives in Syracuse, New York and is Vice-President of Howe & Rusling, an investment management firm based in Rochester, NY.

Printed in the United States
86871LV00005B/500/A